RULE # 6

Velominati.com is one of the world's MOST POPULAR and rapidly growing cycling websites. LAUNCHED IN 2009 to foster a PASSION FOR CYCLING, it boasts a LOYAL readership hailing from all corners of the globe.

THE RULES

The Way of the Cycling Disciple

Velominati

KEEPERS OF THE COG

SCEPTRE

First published in Great Britain in 2013 by Sceptre
An imprint of Hodder & Stoughton
An Hachette UK company

First published in paperback in 2014

1

A CIP catalogue record for this title is available from the British Library.

Paperback ISBN 978 1 444 76753 7
eBook ISBN 978 1 444 76752 0

Printed and bound by Clays Ltd, St Ives plc

Typeset in Gotham Light by Palimpsest Book Production Limited,
Falkirk, Stirlingshire

Hodder & Stoughton policy is to use papers that are natural, renewable
and recyclable products and made from wood grown in sustainable
forests. The logging and manufacturing processes are expected to
conform to the environmental regulations of the country of origin.

Hodder & Stoughton Ltd
338 Euston Road
London NW1 3BH

www.sceptrebooks.co.uk

Contents

Rule #1 // Obey The Rules. **Rule #2** // Lead by example. **Rule #3** // Guide the uninitiated. **Rule #4** // It's all about the bike. **Rule #11** // Family does not come first. The bike does. **Rule #12** // The correct number of bikes to own is n+1. **Rule #13** // If you draw race number 13, turn it upside down. **Rule #24** // Speeds and distances shall be referred to and measured in kilometres. **Rule #25** // The bikes on top of your car should be worth more than the car. **Rule #43** // Don't be a jackass. **Rule #47** // Drink tripels, don't ride triples. **Rule #51** // Livestrong wristbands are cock-rings for your arms. **Rule #58** // Support your local bike shop. **Rule #77** // Respect the earth; don't litter. **Rule #81** // Don't talk it up. **Rule #89** // Pronounce it correctly. **Rule #93** // Descents are not for recovery. Recovery ales are for recovery. **Rule #94** // Use the correct tool for the job, and use the tool correctly.

Rule #6 // Free your mind and your legs will follow. **Rule #20** // There are only three remedies for pain. **Rule #38** // Don't play leapfrog. **Rule #39** // Never ride without your eyewear. **Rule #42** // A bike race shall never be preceded with a swim and/or followed by a run. **Rule #49** // Keep the rubber side down. **Rule #55** // Earn your turns. **Rule #59** // Hold your line. **Rule #63** // Point in the direction you're turning. **Rule #64** // Cornering confidence increases with time and experience. **Rule #67** // Do your time in the wind. **Rule #68** // Rides are to be measured by quality, not quantity. **Rule #79** // Fight for your town lines. **Rule #83** // Be self-sufficient. **Rule #84** // Follow the Code. **Rule #85** // Descend like a Pro. **Rule #86** // Don't half-wheel. **Rule #87** // The ride starts on time. No exceptions. **Rule #88** // Don't surge. **Rule #92** // No sprinting from the hoods.

PART III: The Bike   113

Rule #8 // Saddles, bars and tyres shall be carefully matched. **Rule #26** // Make your bike photogenic. **Rule #29** // No European posterior man-satchels. **Rule #30** // No frame-mounted pumps. **Rule #34** // Mountain bike shoes and pedals have their place. **Rule #40** // Tyres are to be mounted with the label centred over the valve stem. **Rule #41** // Quick-release levers are to be carefully positioned. **Rule #48** // Saddles must be level and pushed back. **Rule #54** // No aerobars on road bikes. **Rule #57** // No stickers. **Rule #60** // Ditch the washer-nut and valve-stem cap. **Rule #61** // Like your guns, saddles should be smooth and hard. **Rule #65** // Maintain and respect your machine. **Rule #66** // No mirrors. **Rule #69** // Cycling shoes and bicycles are made for riding. **Rule #73** // Gear and brake cables should be cut to optimum length. **Rule #74** // V-Meters or small computers only. **Rule #75** // Race numbers are for races.

PART IV: The Aesthete   157

Rule #7 // Tan lines should be cultivated and kept razor sharp. **Rule #14** // Shorts should be black. **Rule #15** // Black shorts should also be worn with leader's jerseys. **Rule #16** // Respect the jersey. **Rule #17** // Team kit is for members of the team. **Rule #18** // Know what to wear.

Don't suffer kit confusion. **Rule #19** // Introduce yourself. **Rule #21** // Cold weather gear is for cold weather. **Rule #22** // Cycling caps are for Cycling. **Rule #23** // Tuck only after reaching Escape Velocity. **Rule #27** // Shorts and socks should be like Goldilocks. **Rule #28** // Socks can be any damn colour you like. **Rule #31** // Spare tubes, multi-tools and repair kits should be stored in jersey pockets. **Rule #32** // Humps are for camels: no hydration packs. **Rule #33** // Shave your guns. **Rule #35** // No visors on the road. **Rule #36** // Eyewear shall be Cycling-specific. **Rule #37** // The arms of the eyewear shall always be placed over the helmet straps. **Rule #44** // Position matters. **Rule #45** // Slam your stem. **Rule #46** // Keep your bars level. **Rule #50** // Facial hair is to be carefully regulated. **Rule #53** // Keep your kit clean and new. **Rule #56** // Espresso or macchiato only. **Rule #62** // You shall not ride with earphones. **Rule #76** // Helmets are to be hung from your stem. **Rule #78** // Remove unnecessary gear. **Rule #80** // Always be Casually Deliberate. **Rule #82** // Close the gap. **Rule #95** // Never lift your bike over your head.

Introduction

// By William Fotheringham

It was snowing the other day, and I wanted to take my daughter outside. She wasn't in the mood. Well, I said, you know how we roll. Rule #5, she replied. She has never ridden a bike in anger.

You can spot a cultural phenomenon in a variety of ways, but the tipping point is when it needs no explanation. When something has truly woven itself into the cultural fabric, you don't need to go through what it is and why. That, rather remarkably, is where the Velominati Rules have got to in many Cycling households, as the episode with my daughter showed. You have Rule #5 moments. You have Rule #5 rides.

We all have our own rules for Cycling, the code by which we operate. I have a friend of long standing who works by the notebook: If you ride like a dick, your name goes in the notebook. The notebook doesn't exist, other than in his mind. But the guy who had attacked us on every club ride for a year definitely went in the notebook. When he finally ended up vulnerable in the windward gutter one day, Serge, as the Velominati would call him, didn't even know he was in the wind until The Man With the Hammer came to call. At which point my friend said sagely, 'He was in the notebook.' The notebook is almost biblical: as you sow, you reap. Eventually. The notebook isn't a list of guys who are going to get a horse's head in the bed. It's way more subtle, more that if you ignore the conventions, you get no sympathy when it backfires on you. In other words: Obey The Rules.

My old mate, needless to say, is an alumnus of the Eddy and Roger School, in which all elements of Cycling conduct are filtered through the same prism: what would Eddy, and/or Roger, have done? Sideburns? Good. Hands on the brake levers, back flat, forearms flat? Good. Tubulars kept in the cellar for 20 years before using? Good. Racing in snow-storms? Obligatory. Drill out your chainrings? Yes. (Apologies, this was the 70s.) The honorary members of the Eddy and Roger School are the hardmen of Cycling, who – guess what? – crop up in these pages: Sean Kelly (the man who I once saw whizzing down an Irish back lane like it was Arenberg, defying zero temperatures, mud and slime to beat a load of amateurs in a Christmas handicap race, because the said race was in his hometown, run by his Cycling club.); Laurent Fignon, whose impeccable cool in the 1984 Tour meant he is the only man to have laughed at Bernard Hinault, in public, and to have survived. And so on. The Tour de France contender who complained that there were too many dangerous descents in the 2011 race was clearly not a student of Eddy and Roger. (We all know who he is.)

At Chez Fotheringham, we also have Rule #5a. That's one I would propose for addition to the Code. It's three words that say it all: Eddy never complained. There are purists who argue that in fact Eddy did complain, frequently, and they have a point. Eddy was known for pointing out to the opposition that he had a headache/sore knee/aching elbow/bit of a cold before the start of a bike race. But he would invariably go on and win said bike race. He wouldn't use the ailment as an excuse to avoid the bike race.

The Rules criss-cross with a more obscure code of conduct called The Knowledge, which will be familiar to those who have studied the wise words of Robert Millar. The Knowledge is a body of European conventions on Cycling which had to be followed by Millar, Sean Yates, Paul Sherwen, Phil Anderson and the other anglophone pioneers of the 1980s, and it was set down by Millar in a couple of Cycle Sport articles in the mid-1990s. You don't eat the middle of the baguette. You never have the air-conditioning on in the hotel room or the team car. You wear a woolly hat at all times when off your bike in all seasons apart from high summer. You always resist the temptation to train in shorts, especially if it's 40 degrees Celsius. You take a shower not a bath, because bathing affects the muscle tone. The Velominati Rule that you never shave the day before a race because it weakens you, is straight out of The Knowledge.

What underpins the Rules, the Knowledge and the Eddy and Roger School is passion. A long time ago, I asked Eddy what drove him to win pretty much every bike race worth pinning a number on for (apart from Paris-Tours, for the pedants among you), and he had a simple answer: passion, only passion. 'It was stronger than me. I was a slave to it.'

The key thing to remember about passion is that the Robert Millar rule applies. The RM rule is that climbers don't suffer less than the rest of us, they suffer the same but go faster uphill. What I mean by that is that passion has many forms, and many levels of intensity, and leads us to different places.

Passion isn't restricted to Eddy and Roger. It's the driver of all sports, and of our sport in particular, because Cycling is not just something we all do at weekends. For many of us it's a lifestyle. And that, I think, is what comes out in these pages.

Passion is the indefinable element that binds us as Cyclists. It's what we have in common with the guys who are good enough at racing their bikes to earn a living from it, to win the races we dream of merely riding. They dreamt too, whether it was Tom Simpson with his posters of Coppi on the wall as a kid, or Eddy picking the sponsor's letter-stitching out of a Faema jersey before his first race. That's what unites them with the kid who dove down the banking onto me at track league the other week to get into the nonexistent gap in front of me. (He's in the notebook.)

I don't often think about the place Cycling holds in my life, but I was made to do so when someone once said to me: 'It must be lovely for you having your hobby as your work'. Hobby? Hobby? I was curiously indignant at the term. Hobby sounds like something casual, something you pick up and drop, something you do in your spare time, something essentially frivolous. Cycling is fun, and, of course, frivolous compared to the serious stuff of life. If push comes to shove, it gets shoved, but it's never felt frivolous to me. I've taken the idea of competing far more seriously than most other things and devoted far more thought to it. I've been unbelievably lucky to have followed that passion in the way I have, to have raced my bike at the mediocre level I have (and still do), to have been able to see bike races close up and look some of the greats of Cycling eye to eye. It's not just been a way of earning a living, although I've been lucky enough to do so.

So what is this thing that consumes our thoughts and many of our waking hours? Sport? Much more than that. Lifestyle? Too clinical. Life, perhaps. As in get one. Please. It's a passion. That's all. And that could be the most important Rule of them all.

William Fotheringham has been cycling correspondent at the London Guardian *since 1994, was a founding editor of* Cycle Sport *and* Procycling *magazines, and has been racing a bike since 1980. His biography of Eddy Merckx,* Merckx: Half-Man, Half-Bike, *was the first cycling book to top the UK bestseller lists. He has also written biographies of Tom Simpson and Fausto Coppi. His latest book is a compilation of* Guardian *articles,* Riding Hard, *published in June 2013.*

Prologue

Cycling is a mighty sport with a rich and complex history. Every racer, company, piece of kit and component has a legend or story behind it – a reason to be passionate for its existence. In many cases it also has a personal and nostalgic connection to our lives.

While steeped in tradition, it is also fiercely modern and seeks advancement through technology and science, a fact that serves only to deepen its complexity.

From this fragile balance between tradition and advancement comes a longstanding sense of etiquette. The modes of acceptable behavior for the Cyclist have evolved alongside the sport's elements of danger and the necessary dependence on fellow riders, which produce a complex web of what is and what is not acceptable, spanning the spectrum from the purely aesthetic to the purely functional.

We are the Velominati, sacred Order of the Cycling Disciple. We spend our days poring over the essence of Cycling to understand how it makes up the sport's colorful fabric. This is the Velominati's raison d'être.

La Vie Velominatus is a term that the Velominati use to express the Life of the Cycling Disciple: one who holds the sport, its history, its culture, its etiquette and its practice in a nearly religious context. *La Vie* translates from French into English as the life, but to refer only to the life is to focus on just one facet of its meaning; it is to ignore the community of the many like-minded souls with whom we share this beautiful experience.

A life is for the individual; the Way is for the collective. This is the Way of the Cycling Disciple.

La Vie Velominatus is centered on passion fueled through five principal aspects.

First, we believe that the best way to become a better Cyclist is to ride your bike as often as possible, as seriously as possible.

Second, we hold the history of Cycling in reverence. We admire those who have come before us and who have suffered for us. We view the current culture of Cycling with the same humility as those upon whose shoulders we stand.

Third, we approach the sport with the wisdom that evolution is the key to survival: that the way we have done things before is not necessarily the way we should do them in the future. We love tradition, but we embrace the future.

Fourth, we believe that aesthetics build the motivation to practice the sport in a manner necessary to become the best, to ride day after day, season after rainy season, year after year. If you look good, you feel good. As Paul Fournel says, to look good is already to go fast.

Fifth, and most importantly, we believe that in order to best achieve the first four aspects, you need a healthy and possibly sinister sense of humor.

The Rules form one of the pillars of *La Vie Velominatus*.

While the Way extends far beyond a list of items that, at face value, may seem arbitrary or obtuse to the common observer, The Rules serve as an induction into the fundamental principles of living life as a Cyclist. While some may seem arbitrary and others purely aesthetic, all are rooted in the history, culture and etiquette of our sport and are intended for one purpose only: to inspire people to ride their bikes more often and love them more deeply than they do now.

You will quickly find that chief among The Rules is Rule #5: Harden the Fuck Up. This element is central to the Way; we refer to its essence as The V (pronounced "The Five"). Cycling is hard, and it requires that we are tough in response. The V is in every one of us, like a deep well to draw from when we need it most. It penetrates us, it surrounds us, it holds our sport together.

There are those among the Velominati who hold Rule #5 in such esteem that they feel all other Rules are superfluous. These Rule #5 Fundamentalists may have a point, though to reduce it to such simplicity misses the greater theme that there is endless pleasure to be found in complexity. While a glass of water can quench a thirst more refreshingly than anything else, a fine wine sets itself apart from others through its depth of flavor and originality. We choose to embrace the wisdom imparted by the other Rules – to relish training in bad weather (see Rule #9), to frequent our local bike shops rather than to shop online (see Rule #58) and to seek to always be Casually Deliberate (see Rule #80). Indeed, the Velominati seek to distinguish ourselves by devouring the subtlety of this glorious sport.

This book will assume nothing but passion – whether it be

dormant or vibrant. We will not give history lessons, we will not explain what a quick-release skewer is. There are other resources much better suited to explaining such things or the intricacies of training or pedaling technique.

On the contrary, this book will aim to inspire you to climb on your bike; whether you last climbed aboard yesterday or a decade ago. We hope to help you discover the same love and curiosity for the sport, the bicycle and this life – *La Vie Velominatus* – that we have. This is an endless spring of motivation, enjoyment and pleasure that serves to inspire us to continue to ride, to learn more of our sport, and to become not just better Cyclists, but better people.

The Rules and our Lexicon have evolved organically over the years, and what we have today is a list of ninety-five Rules. The Rules are numbered chronologically as they were added to the canon – not by order of importance. For this reason, we have chosen to group The Rules into five sections based on theme rather than leaving them in the order in which they appear on Velominati.com. They do, however, retain their original numbered names. Over the years, we have developed a unique vocabulary; should a term's meaning escape your understanding, consult the Lexicon at the back of this book or with the community at Velominati.com.

Vive la Vie Velominatus.

PART I:
The Disciple

It has been a long, gradual process, this journey to become a Disciple of Cycling. Perhaps it began with the sensation of flight the first time we got a bicycle to move forward without wobbling about and falling over. Or perhaps it was the first time we changed the tape on a set of handlebars and marvelled at how fresh the machine looked. Or maybe it was the first time we noticed a familiar heaviness, a sense of loss even, if for reasons beyond our control we were faced with time away from our bicycles.

Cycling is a difficult sport. Not difficult in the way getting your head kicked in playing rugby or American football might be difficult. Not difficult like trying to keep from drowning in a swimming pool is difficult. Not difficult like trying to hit a ball with a stick is difficult. It is difficult in the sense that our rides are measured in hours and hundreds of kilometres. It is difficult in the sense that the greatest obstacle is not the bike or the terrain, but our mind: we must withstand the temptation to stay indoors when the rain slashes down, have the courage to continue when our legs ache, and exhibit sufficient fortitude to endure bitter cold, stifling heat and everything in between.

Cyclists think differently from other people. We strive to scale the highest mountain passes in the shortest possible time; we hunger to propel ourselves down the narrowest, roughest Northern European farm lanes. We pull back the curtain to peer out at the dark clouds and rain-sodden roads and hurry to gather our kit, the quicker to submit ourselves to the savage glory of The Ride.

When a Cyclist speaks of 'feeling great', we mean a different thing than most people do. The Cycling Disciple must learn to control their efforts even as their lungs threaten to explode and the heart attempts to leap from its confining ribcage. This while the body is bathed with so much lactic acid that our jawbone begins to ache, the guns become burning lumps of coal and our eyesight falters.

To still push to go *just a bit* faster, to us, is 'feeling great'.

Cycling has a rich and complex history. Every company, racer, piece of kit, and component has a legend behind it. In many cases they also have a personal and nostalgic connection to our lives. Visions of our heroes – the feats of Merckx, Coppi, Hinault – fly through our minds as we race our shadows up a mountain or stare at our reflections in the Flemish Mirror of rain-soaked tarmac.

While the sport is steeped in tradition, though, it is also fiercely modern, a fact that serves only to deepen its complexity. We are inspired by past legends, but what ultimately drives us is progress: lighter, stiffer equipment, more breathable clothing that is better able to deal with moisture, whether it be from our bodies or from the heavens. Yet none of these advancements are taken at face value; all are measured in the context of our great sport and the path we have collectively ridden.

This duality gives us perspective and helps us to grow

without forgetting our roots. It allows us to recognise that a Velominatus is a Cycling Disciple of the highest order. We spend our days poring over the very essence of what makes ours such a special sport and how that spirit weaves into Cycling's colourful fabric. This is the Velominati's raison d'être. This is our agony – our badge of honour – our sin.

Eddy Merckx, The Prophet, hands down The V-estament.

RULE #1 //
OBEY
THE RULES

1969 Ronde van Vlaanderen – In perhaps his strongest season ever, Merckx rode at the front of the field in a wet and rainy Ronde van Vlaanderen with a cozy 80km left to race. Riding solo into a driving wind, his director instructed him to back off and wait for the bunch. 'Go screw yourself,' was the Prophet's response. Merckx was parting the waters on the road to Mt. Velomis; no one would stand in the way of his destiny.

An ancient Velominati legend:

> He stood high upon Mount Velomis, half man, half bike. As He gazed down at the world that He had worked so hard to build, He realised that His Disciples had become soft.

> They complained of cold, of rain, of dangerous descents. They complained of wind, of heat, of long days in the saddle. They rode in worn out, mismatched kit, with European Posterior Man-Satchels loosely swaying beneath their saddles. Their machines in disrepair, they disgraced all He stood for.

> And so it was, high upon Mount Velomis, that He climbed once more upon His bike. And as the wheels began slowly to hum again upon His mighty rollers, He began to pedal, first in desperation, then in anger, then in benevolence.

> When His fire had finally melted into compassion, and the sweat began to pour from His Mighty Guns onto the ancient rock beneath Him, the Spirits cast into the very stone of Mount Velomis, The Rules.

Mount Velomis rises like Olympus above a century of history, a culture of tradition and etiquette of Cycling, from the early exploits of Major Taylor and Henri Desgrange to the deifying feats of Coppi, Bobet, Merckx and Hinault. Its shadow casts long over the invention of the quick release, the derailleur – all things we now take for granted in our great sport. The lessons learned through the collective experience of every bike mechanic paired to each of their demanding and micromanaging riders cascade down like rivers off its slopes. The ferocious storm of the Cyclist's heart burns as we push ourselves beyond what we believe we can do.

When a Cyclist kits up and climbs aboard their bike, they aren't standing on the shoulders of giants; they stand upon a towering mountain of history and legend. They stand upon the mighty rock of Mount Velomis.

We are Cyclists. The rest of the world merely rides a bike.

Obey the Rules.

RULE #2 //
LEAD BY EXAMPLE

It is forbidden for someone familiar with The Rules to knowingly assist another person to breach them.

It has been said by some or all of us at some point that while we make The Rules, we don't have to abide by them. Sounds a bit like an excuse used by a busted doper, really: 'Yeah I took drugs and lied about it, but I had to do it because everyone else was doing it'. No one is buying that, so stop trying to sell it. So if a good friend asks for advice on whether or not a helmet mirror should be employed, you instinctively know the correct answer.

But what if that same friend really *wants* the helmet mirror, or has been strongly encouraged by their loved ones that they would feel more secure if they attached such a monstrosity to their head, no matter how uncool it looks? Is the argument that you'll just look like a dork when getting crushed from behind by a semi versus *not* looking like a dork when getting crushed from behind by a semi really the best defence? Or do you just say 'Sure, stick it on, if it makes you feel safer, or prevents you sleeping on the couch for an indefinite period because you went against the wishes of your better half?'

Yes, you know the answer. We must protect our fellow Velominati not from trucks or cars or even spouses: we must protect them from going out there in immaculate kit, bike clean and perfectly tuned, and spoiling it all by some act of madness like donning a Yellow Jacket of Authority (YJA) or helmet mirror just because of a perceived safety benefit. You must strongly insist that such items have no place in their wardrobe or kit, and that they risk admonishment from the rest of the riding group (who will no doubt be well versed in such matters already, if you have been fulfilling your duty to the utmost of your ability). If they still insist, then you must raise your hands in resignation and declare that you'll have no further part in the matter. In a few weeks' or months' time when the offender has seen the error of their ways, the forthcoming apology and thanks will be enough. You can quietly and humbly bask in the knowledge that you upheld your end of the bargain, and sanity and good taste have prevailed once more.

RULE #3 //
GUIDE THE UNINITIATED

No matter how good you think your reason is to knowingly breach The Rules, it is never good enough.

To the uninitiated The Rules often seem arbitrary and arcane. But to the Velominatus, The Rules have meaning and provide a path to achieving Cycling enlightenment. However solitary our riding lives may be, we will inevitably cross paths with other Cyclists. Rule #3 addresses the responsibility we have to our sport to lead other Cyclists down that path as we ride it ourselves.

Adherence to Rule #3 requires that we first recognise that nobody and everybody created The Rules. The Rules were divined at the altar of the road and forged in the crucible of Cycling tradition by those who have come before us. For Merckx's sake, do not dare to suppose that The Rules are merely about style or vanity. Furthermore, do not think for one second that these truths, born of necessity and recorded for posterity, have not been tested over millions of kilometres on roads passing over cobblestones, mountain passes, and windswept fields. This collective wisdom is what gives The Rules power, for they are greater than our sum and represent decades of pain and suffering on the bike. Once this is realised, the common knee-jerk criticism of The

Rules being 'roadie snobbery' is rendered utterly ignorant. Plainly stated, your helmet straps (see Rule #37) and tyre labels (see Rule #40) are that way for good reason, and that reason is also what makes those things look Awesome.

Rule #3 is a call to duty for the Velominatus. In essence, it says that once we've been shown the way by those who have gone before us, we must guide others as they embark on their journey. Notice, though, that Rule #3 does not stipulate *how* we go about guiding others. One may choose to be brash and firm in pointing out their discretions. This method is persuasive for those who see the world in black and white, those who may tend toward the path of the Cognoscenti. But in this approach one runs the risk of violating Rule #43 (Don't be a Jackass) or – worse – turning the Pedalwan away from The Path. One may conversely choose the Socratic Method and in so doing become a Cycling Sensei, enabling the learner to discover their own internal motivation to walk The Path. The risk here is in imparting vagaries or, Merckx forbid, a lack of discipline and thus rendering The Rules somehow 'optional'. In either case, guiding the uninitiated will harden your resolve and reaffirm that you are riding the correct path yourself.

RULE #4 //
IT'S ALL ABOUT THE BIKE

It is, absolutely, without question, unequivocally, about the bike. Anyone who says otherwise is obviously a twat-waffle.

'If a bike can be sexy, that one definitely is.'

I was standing proudly next to my newly built machine, one I had dreamed of throwing a leg over for close to five years. The curation of the steed, down to its most elementary components, had been laboriously considered and selected before being reconsidered and replaced by another long before the time ever came to actually start acquiring any of the bits. So hell yes, a bike can be sexy. And hell yes, this one was.

Much can change in the time it takes to build a bike. It had taken me over five years to finally obtain the one I was flaunting to my friends that day. Technology, the equipment that my idols rode, the paint schemes of the frame – all these things had shifted like Flandrian mud running between rain-soaked cobblestones.

Selecting a component is a decision that must be laboured over for weeks or months, revisited vigorously and discussed in detail with anyone too polite to walk away. Even when so doing, an error is sometimes made and the part must be exchanged for the one that feels better in hand or balances the aesthetic of the bike more evenly.

This doesn't even touch on critical elements such as what size frame to purchase. As a boy I had always ridden bicycles that were too large; my intention being to grow into them as I made my slow journey towards adulthood (I'm told that I'm still not there). I wasn't keen on buying yet another too-large frame, but going too small is a problem without remedy. Months of laborious thought were therefore devoted to this crucial decision, supported by the unearthing of high-school geometry and trigonometry books, which provided essential assistance in determining which frame sizes would offer the right lengths, heights and angles to assist in elevating me from donkey to thoroughbred.

Even the details that are easily changed at later times warrant lengthy consideration for the simple fact that when the machine is first built, it will burn that first impression into your psyche for an eternity. If you were to inadvertently choose the wrong colour bar wrap or saddle, it would leave a taste in your mouth that is not easily washed away (though a nice hoppy ale is a good way to start).

Careful thought was given to the weight of a component versus its cost and durability. As a tall, lanky fellow, flex is of primary concern, yet the weight of the bike is something I'm not eager to increase given the considerable aggregate weight of rider and machine. The challenge of balancing these factors is reminiscent of trying to stay upright on my first ride without the guiding hand of my father on the back of the saddle.

This particular bicycle lived in my heart for half a decade before I ever touched any of its tubes. Since owning it, it lives and grows with me, is adapted to suit my evolution as a rider and, like any tool, to meet the demands of particular roads. Wheels are selected for climbing, cobblestones, or training rides. Handlebar tape is padded to ease the inevitability of fatigued hands on the pavé. Cassettes are swapped out depending on the grade and undulations of the road. And perhaps most importantly, tyres are chosen for tread pattern and width depending on where the tarmac, gravel or stones may carry me. In the end this bike will live on in my heart long after it has departed to the solemn dustbin high upon the slopes of Mount Velomis.

If I devoted a quarter of the thought I put into the curating and maintenance of my bicycle to my job – or the development of my character, for that matter – I'd be an unstoppable force in the world.

But I can't be bothered with all that – it's all about the bike.

RULE #11 //
FAMILY DOES NOT COME FIRST.
THE BIKE DOES

Sean Kelly, being interviewed after the '84 Amstel Gold Race, spots his wife leaning against his Citroën AX. He interrupts the interview to tell her to get off the paintwork, to which she shrugs, 'In your life the car comes first, then the bike, then me.' Instinctively, he snaps back, 'You got the order wrong. The bike comes first.'

First, some background on Sean Kelly.

Sean Kelly never smiled during his career, not even on the many occasions that he crossed the finish line as victor. Seven virgins in nine countries fainted simultaneously on the one occasion he allowed himself to momentarily stop scowling.

Sean Kelly famously rode frames built by the French framebuilder, Vitus. Lovely frames made of lugged aluminium or carbon-Kevlar tubes, what they lacked in rigidity they more than made up for in beauty. His teammates were each issued a frame for training and a frame for racing. Sean Kelly ate these frames whole, each one lasting only a single race before being retired to the scrapheap.

Sean Kelly is an honest, hard-working, straight-talking Irishman, the distillation of the essential elements that make Cycling great. In retirement, he has become a comparatively jovial lad, as I'm given to understand that he occasionally chuckles, though if his words are coated with anything, it's still piss and vinegar.

Sean Kelly raises his arms in triumph as he beats Greg LeMond to the line in the 1986 edition of Milan-Sanremo.

Born in rural Ireland in the mid-50s, he was raised on hard work and dedication. He abandoned his vocation as a farm hand and instead chose to pursue his destiny as one of the most formidable competitors our sport has ever known.

If one expression speaks of the luck of the Irish and another of luck favouring the prepared, then surely Kelly leaned more towards the latter than the former. Relentlessly devoted to his trade and wholly lacking of a sense of humour, this man was not to be trifled with.

Kelly turned pro in the 70s and systematically dismantled every rider whose back wheel crossed through his gaze. A simple man raised on hard work in hard lands, he pinned little worth on progress and the evolution of Cycling kit. Long after the whole of the peloton had migrated to the clipless pedal, Kelly's position in the bunch could instantly be identified by the glint of sunlight reflecting off the toe clips he stubbornly refused to abandon.

The 1992 edition of Milano Sanremo saw Italian Moreno Argentin ride across the summit of the famous Poggio alone on his way to a certain victory; just three kilometres of twisting urban descent lay ahead before a single, flat kilometre that led to the finish on the Via Roma in Sanremo.

There was just one problem: Sean Kelly was behind, and Sean Kelly doesn't mess around. What's more, Sean Kelly knows brakes are for sissies, and Sean Kelly ain't no sissy. Argentin descended like he'd stolen something and didn't want to go to jail. Sean Kelly descended like he'd rather die than lose. Kelly caught the Italian in the final kilometre and beat him with a Casually Deliberate glance before they even entered the final sprint.

For seventeen long years, Sean Kelly took wins from deserving riders of the highest pedigree. From the beginning to the twilight of his career, he won races through cunning, strength, hardness and unwavering determination. But mostly he took his wins through total and complete dedication to his craft.

For him, there was nothing but the bike. Family did not come first, the bike did.

RULE #12 //
THE CORRECT
NUMBER OF BIKES TO
OWN IS N+1

While the minimum number of bikes one should own is three, the correct number is n+1, where n is the number of bikes currently owned. This equation may also be rewritten as s−1, where s is the number of bikes owned that would result in separation from your partner.

I'm in the market for a new cyclo-cross bike. My partner is supportive of this, despite knowing I already have a cyclo-cross bike. Not to mention three road bikes, a commuter and a mountain bike. Being a Cyclist herself, she naturally has three road bikes of her own, as well as cyclocross and mountain bikes.

Nevertheless, she holds a controlling vote on the Budget Committee, and all such purchases need to pass through said committee. What our system lacks in bureaucracy, it makes up for in scrutiny; it's fair to say I'm relieved to have gained committee approval.

In fact, she's excited. The frame-builder in question is a local Pacific Northwest boutique and the Pacific Northwest is all about boutique. After a lengthy discussion of whether a Gruppo, Group-San or Broset should grace this particular steed, she uttered a phrase that caused my heart to leap into my throat: 'After this, I assume we can put the bike-purchase thing to rest for a bit and focus on some of our other priorities, right?' It wasn't a question, even though it was phrased as one.

Visions of the 29er and time-trial bikes flew through my mind as I rushed to agree. To be honest, I'm not opposed to focusing on 'other' priorities. But truth be told, I am at a loss to understand what she means by this turn of phrase. I thought the 29er and TT bikes *were* the other priorities.

The Velominati love our bikes. The bike is more than a tool in our trade; each machine we ride helps us find a connection to The V that leaves an indelible mark upon our spirit. We take no bike for granted, and we understand that a bicycle unridden is a bicycle not cherished – and that a bicycle not cherished is perhaps the saddest thing imaginable.

Nevertheless, we always crave another bike. Perhaps it is an ancient derangement of a polygamous hunter-gatherer heritage; perhaps it is an artifact of the Stockholm syndrome we find ourselves in where we attach an otherworldly value to a machine that does little more than cause us to primitively suffer.

Each bicycle that enters my stable is one carefully curated and assembled. I worked the entire summer between sixth and seventh grade doing odd jobs to buy my first real race bike. Shortly after its purchase, I began customising it; I mounted a Cinelli stem and Scott Drop-In bars, which I wrapped in Benotto bar tape, if you can call something without adhesive 'bar tape'. Shortly thereafter, I purchased a set of Time pedals and soon after that, a Selle San Marco Regal saddle. In the few short months I had owned the bike, it was transformed into something unrecognisable from the machine I had wheeled off the floor of the local bike shop.

I loved that bike. I rode it until it fell apart. When it fell apart, I repaired it, or bought parts to replace those rendered unsalvageable. I rode it for nearly twenty years, and some of its components even live out in hospice on one of my current bicycles.

Each bike I've owned since has started as a frame purchase and evolved into a glorious steed, each with a tale that speaks of long waits and squeezed budgets.

In 2003, my Velomihottie and I rode l'Etape du Tour, a yearly event put on by the organisation of the Tour de France that allows civilians to race a particular mountain stage of that year's Tour. That year, the route took us over the stage from Pau to Bayonne, outside Biarritz, France. The course profile spoke of 220km over three passes before an 80-kilometre downhill stretch from the top of the final pass to the finish. We trained as hard as we were able to in the spring leading up the event; days of 200 or more kilometres littered our training diaries.

A few days after completing the event, we returned to the route to watch the Tour race the same roads. We spectated on the road before retreating into a café in the French boonies appropriately called the Calamity Jane, where we watched the remainder of the stage on a television whose antennae required constant attention from the bar staff and coaxed cheers from the patronage whenever a clear picture was produced. Tyler Hamilton won that day aboard a proto-type bicycle that would later become the Cervelo R3.

For seven years, I dreamed of owning a bike like the one Hamilton had ridden to victory on the roads we had briefly shared, his admitted doping notwithstanding.

When the day finally came for me to throw my leg over the top tube of my very own R3, it was as though I was reborn. The culmination of so many dreams, converging upon that very moment, is perhaps best described by what mathematicians refer to as a 'singularity', a single point where physical principles as we understand them cease to hold sway over the events as we witness them. Divide by Zero, to put it in calculator terms.

A friend of mine built the frame that I currently ride and race and which introduced me to perhaps the most vulgar and elementary form of bicycles racing, cyclo-cross. Combine bike racing, trail running, miniature golf and fight club into a single sport and you're halfway there. Add some mud and booze and you're starting to get the picture. I love the bike I'm racing now and it's one of a kind; photos from the races I contest always reveal a giant orange frame being shouldered a metre above every other frame on the run-up.

It has, however, endured some trauma induced by my incompetence as a cyclo-crosser and also suffers from being a rather weighty thing. When it comes to Cycling, I've made the conclusion that while I'm allowed to be heavy, my bike isn't.

In a sport that involves lifting your bicycle several dozen times during a race, I am keen for a feathery machine. Which brings me back to the opening sentiment: I'm in the market for a cyclo-cross frame.

And after that cools off, I'll be in the market for a 29er and time-trial bike. And after all that, I still won't have any bikes made of titanium. And if I get a 29er, it will be either a hardtail or a full-suspension bike, which means I won't have either a full-suspension bike or a hardtail. And I doubt any of those will be titanium.

I hear titanium rides great, and that a titanium bike is the last bike you'll ever need to buy. Whoever said that obviously has no idea what they're going on about. Where does *need* come into it?

RULE #13 //
IF YOU DRAW RACE
NUMBER 13,
TURN IT UPSIDE DOWN

Paradoxically, the same mind that holds such control over the body is also woefully fragile and prone to superstitious thoughts. It fills easily with doubt and is distracted by ancillary details. This is why the tape must always be perfect, the machine silent, the kit spotless. And, if you draw the unlucky Number 13, turn it upside down to counteract its negative energy.

When I raced Nordic skis, we dealt with an enormous amount of cold and grey weather. We naturally had loads of kit to combat these situations. Thicker gloves, lighter gloves, mediumer gloves. Thicker hats, lighter hats, mediumer hats. Sunny sunnies, overcast sunnies, rainy sunnies, (which weren't sunnies as much as yellow-coloured glasses). I had skis for soft snow, skis for hard snow, and skis for in-between snow.

I trained for hours and hours – more than anyone else in my group. I spent my summers training much harder than any of my competitors, mostly because summer training was how I discovered my love for the bike.

I rode my bike through all the months that didn't see snow on the roads. We trained on mountain-bike trails in Northern

Minnesota, the likes of which few people have ever ridden. One year, we invited a rival coach to train with us for a day. It poured rain and we rode our usual singletrack, which featured heavy, shin-cutting underbrush along trails so steep and rocky we routinely snapped chains and bent handlebars.

He threw his bike into the brush on more than one occasion – partly in rage and partly just for the excuse to have a rest while he fetched it.

When he returned from this ride, he reportedly told his team to forget about winning the major races that year; if that was how I trained, then I had them all sorted.

The fact is, that *wasn't* how I trained. We gave Rick a Tourist's Ride. With him, we rode one of the four legs of the trail. It took us six or seven hours. During the summer, we routinely rode all four legs at once. Usually in eight hours or less.

This wasn't mountain-biking like we talk about these days; this was an early induction into Wilderness Rule #5 Aided by Bicycle. We would spend entire days on a single hill, trying to see who could get to the top first. These were steep, technical ascents, which we did on fixed steel frames like the Bridgestone MB-1. We labelled each climb as either a Zero, One or Two. If none of us had yet made it all the way up, it was a Zero. If one of us made it, it became a One. If two of us made it, it became a Two. At that point we stopped caring about it and it became a matter of saving face to make it up.

In addition to that, we trained on the road any time we weren't in the forest trying to one-up each other on the dirt.

When the winter came, I transferred my energies into piling hour upon hour in training and preparing for the next race.

The more miserable the conditions the better; frigid conditions were the best, though it fought a close battle with shin-deep snow.

Yet, despite all my training, I knew that all my best races had been contested wearing the same pair of gloves and dark lenses in my Oakley Razors. After a few seasons, I found myself always reaching for the same gloves and lenses whenever there was something at stake; after those countless hours of training, it still came down to the superstition of which gloves and sunnies I wore on race day.

This is perhaps the most peculiar aspect of the Athlete. We train our bodies, knowing that each hour spent working on our fitness represents a deposit into the V-Bank, which will pay its dividends at some later time, when needed.

Yet as Cyclists, we refer to our legs in the third person: 'The legs'. These are otherworldly objects; maybe we have a few sets hanging in the garage and on any given day we take down a pair, mount them and hope they are Good Legs.

Despite our training and our confidence, there is a certain element of our training that goes uncharted by doctors and science; it is the paranormal element, which the Athlete believes exists and which, for that very fact, is real. Voodoo doesn't work until you believe it does, after all.

Have a look around the pro bunch, and pick out the rider who wears race number 13. Notice anything strange about them? Five will get you ten, they pinned it on upside down to counter its unlucky effect.

The Athlete is a beautifully superstitious creature.

RULE #24 //
SPEEDS AND DISTANCES SHALL BE REFERRED TO AND MEASURED IN
KILOMETRES

This includes while discussing Cycling in the workplace with your non-Cycling co-workers, serving to further mystify our sport in the web of their Neanderthalic cognitive capabilities. As the confused expression spreads across their unibrowed faces, casually mention your shaved legs. All of Cycling's monuments are measured in the metric system and as such the English system is forbidden.

Partway between Paris and Roubaix; headed for Roubaix.

Most of the correct-thinking world will come to comply with Rule #24 naturally and honestly. This Rule is directed toward the Velominati in the two or so countries left in the world that wrongly use the imperial system for measuring speed and distance. Aside from the psychological benefit of kilometres rather than miles and kph vs mph making it seem like you're riding both further and faster, all of the monuments are measured in K's. Milan–Sanremo wouldn't be Milan–Sanremo if it were a 185-mile course. OK, it would be, but it is a 298-kilometre course and far be it from the Velominatus to think, let alone speak, of it any differently.

Abiding by this Rule goes beyond allowing the Velominatus to reference pro races in the proper context. When employed on the bike, Rule #24 enables the Cycling Disciple to measure oneself against the rest of the Cycling world. This can be quite helpful for both training and bluffing about your riding exploits at work, in a café or at the pub. Think of the blowhard after the Tuesday-night group ride bragging about his 500k week and 37kph average speed on his solo double century. As he spouts numbers you can smile wryly, nod in affirmation and lie about how you only got out for a 75k spin that week. Next Tuesday, as you do every other Tuesday and after a 500k-week of your own, you drop him on the first slight incline, leaving him to wonder how you can train so little and ride so hard. Now think of the attractive co-worker who is curious about Cycling and takes an interest in you because you ride. The co-worker mentions to you in the break room that she/he went on a ten-mile bike ride on Saturday, looks to you for approval and asks if you rode at all over the weekend. Again, you flash a wry smile, nod in the affirmative and tell the truth about how you went for a 140k training ride in the hills around town on Sunday before lunch. While the co-worker suspects that is good they don't take offence because you didn't one-up them; they don't know what a 'k' is and you just added to their sense of mystery and intrigue about Cycling.

RULE #25 //
THE BIKES ON TOP OF
YOUR CAR
SHOULD BE WORTH MORE
THAN THE CAR

Or at least be relatively more expensive. Basically, if you're putting your Huffy on your Rolls, you're in trouble, mister. Remember what Sean said.

Aside from my shaved legs, social awkwardness and unusual appearance, I stood out in high school by virtue of the horrible state of my car. It was a 1980 diesel Oldsmobile station wagon whose colour closely resembled that of a giant turd. I lovingly called it 'The Brownie'.

I'm not an engineer, so I'm not clear about the nuances, but I'm given to understand that a diesel engine functions on a different principle than that of the common gasoline engine. Rather than relying on a spark to ignite the fuel, a diesel uses pressure in conjunction with glow plugs to bring the fuel to the point of igniting. This difference between a gasoline and diesel engine is most clearly demonstrated by the fact that any time the temperature drops below -10C, a gasoline engine will still start, while a diesel engine won't.

Once started, however, the car was not dissimilar to other

cars; it used several gears for forward locomotion and one for reverse. It also featured a brake pedal should you wish to stop the thing again once you'd managed to get it going. It also had a gas pedal that had the effect of causing the car to emit an enormous black cloud of exhaust and creep to highway speed at an agonisingly slow pace.

The Brownie had a bit of a corrosion problem, brought on by salt the Department of Transportation deposited on the roads in huge quantities whether there was ice on the roads or not. The brown paint of the car was an advantage as it was the same colour as the rust; so long as you stood at a sufficient distance and squinted the right way, the car looked immaculate. This justified my decision to not maintain the vehicle in any way, despite my dad's insistence that I take precautionary measures such as changing the oil and washing it on occasion.

After a few years under my care, the rust patch over the front windshield developed to the point that it let volumes of water through. This wouldn't have bothered me were it not for the fact that the water had nowhere to go but inside the cabin. The obvious solution was to cover the front of the car with duct tape, which worked very well except for the fact that this represented a kind of maintenance in its own right and was in violation of my stated goal of not performing any maintenance on the car in the first place.

I loved that car. It carried me to some of the most amazing experiences of my youth. I routinely loaded my bikes on or inside it (depending on how many people were involved) and drove off to the hills or the woods to spend countless hours doing what I loved most: ride.

The Dutch have an expression that something will come

either from the length or the width. This is to say that your means are given by a rectangle of uniform area; if you make one end longer, you will make the other end shorter. In other words, with a fixed amount of money at your disposal, you can either spend it on your bike or on your car. For the Velominatus, this works out to be a fairly easy decision: we invest only enough money in our car for it to carry us to our next ride.

RULE #43 //
DON'T BE A
JACKASS

But if you absolutely must be a jackass, be a funny jackass. Always remember, we're all brothers and sisters on the road.

Jokes, teasing, laughter and Cycling belong together.

Nobody ever looked at a bike and said to themselves, 'I want to ride that because it will make me an asshole.' We all started to ride bikes because we wanted to have fun. From the youngest toddler on their first balance bike to the always-the-bridesmaid, never-the-bride pro, the point is to go out and have some fun. It's about the feeling we get that is about as close to flying as we can come under our own power. Sure, for most of us our attitudes toward Cycling have evolved over the years to include things like fitness goals, competition, transportation, environmental stewardship or even making a living. At the root of it all, though, was wanting to have fun by escaping our limitations as bipeds.

The person who personifies this Rule the most in the modern era is without a doubt George Hincapie. Beyond being a loyal lieutenant on nine winning Tour teams and an accomplished Spring Classics rider in his own right, Hincapie was regarded as one of the nicest, most approachable riders in the pro peloton. Unlike two of the captains he rode for, Hincapie seems to have remained true to his nature in spite of the pressures and demands that often accompany success. We look to pros for guidance and inspiration for many of The Rules; for Rule #43, one need look no further than Big George.

Of course, roadies have (often deservedly) gained quite the reputation for being jackasses. For reasons not entirely understood, sometimes when people begin to look good and ride well on really nice bikes they think it then becomes acceptable to treat other Cyclists like shit. Poor behaviour – ranging from the relatively small indiscretion of nod-snobbing other riders to more egregious offences like publicly dressing someone's hard-earned bike down – will serve to support the road-snob stereotype. If you find yourself needing to give feedback due to a Rule violation, do it with a sense of humour. At the very least keep yourself in check and do it with a smile.

If you ever feel inclined to behave in a way unbecoming a Velominatus, you are urged to recall the movie *Breaking*

Away. Remember when the Italian pro team came to town to race and Dave, in his exuberance, was able to ride with them in the front while speaking their native tongue? If you do, then you'll remember the Italian rider jamming a frame-mounted pump into Dave's front wheel, causing him to crash out. That guy was a jackass. And he wasn't even funny. Sure, this was a turning point in a fictional movie with fictional characters but it doesn't mean it couldn't happen. Don't be a jackass. Remember the point here is to welcome more people into La Vie Velominatus, not turn them away.

RULE #47 //
DRINK TRIPELS, DON'T RIDE TRIPLES

Cycling and beer are so intertwined we may never understand the full relationship. Beer is a recovery drink, an elixir for post-ride trash-talking and a just plain excellent thing to pour down the neck. We train to drink so don't fool around. Drink quality beer from real breweries. If it is brewed with rice instead of malted barley or requires a lime, you are off the path. Know your bittering units like you know your gear length. Life is short; don't waste it on piss beer.

Just as West Flanders in Belgium is the spiritual home of Cycling, it is also the spiritual home of beer. Sure, the Czechs may have invented pilsner, and the Americans 'Lite Beer', but to enjoy a true beer experience, you really need to look to Belgium.

For any Ves_minatus worth their malt, the ritual of peeling off a sweaty chamois after a long session of serving up lashings of Rule #5 and pouring a beer into a V-Pint is as much a part of the ride as shifting gears, or dropping triathletes. We think about it as we ride, the lure of hops infiltrating our subconscious as we battle wind, rain and gravity, spurred by a promise to ourselves that the sooner we conquer our demons, the sooner we will be able to look back on our victories and savour the reward. We can almost taste it.

As we take care to prepare and maintain our machines, our kit and our bodies, we must also be vigilant in exhibiting the same principles of good taste when it comes to beer. Just as components like chains and cassettes are chosen for quality, so too are our brews carefully selected for the key ingredients that make our post-ride recovery sessions more than just a refuelling. The amount and types of hops and malts, the brewing process, the alcohol content are all important factors to consider. Price should never come into the equation. You don't buy the cheapest no-name chain to save some pennies only to have it break after a couple of hundred kilometres, and you shouldn't buy a 24-pack of weak, watery beer just to save some dollars. Both the chain and the slab won't make it to the end of their lives.

The Velominatus doesn't drink to get drunk. We drink to savour the experience, to imbibe the oldest known nectar of Awesomeness in history, to complement the undertaking of the ride, to celebrate the conquering of the terrain, the pain and the ninnies with their compact cranks, or worse, triples. They will be left to suffer with tasteless, soulless generic faux beers, drinking like they spin out their low gears, left with emptiness and regret for not stepping up and looking into the eye of the great men of Belgium who never once considered anything less than a 53t or a 7%.

RULE #51 //
LIVESTRONG WRISTBANDS
ARE COCKRINGS
FOR YOUR ARMS

While we hate cancer, isn't it better to just donate some money and not have to advertise the fact for the next five years? You may as well get 'try-hard wanker' tattooed on your forehead.

From the day this Rule was penned to the present, so much has transpired. Stuff that the informed, the passionate, already knew. Stuff that the general public, the gullible, those who need something, anything, to attach their own personal dreams and hopes to didn't know. And still, in some cases, refuse to accept.

These poor souls – they *believed*. They were continually told by their hero that miracles do indeed happen, and like new recruits to Scientology, giddy and brainwashed by a barrage of lies, they bought it. They bought the story, the dream, the hope; and they bought the merchandise. The most ubiquitous of which was the little yellow rubber bracelet. If you wore one of these, it said to others two things: I'm a Cyclist, and I believe in miracles. That these miracles don't exist came as a shock to some, but not to those who knew the machinations of professional Cycling and the fact that the Messiah wasn't all he was cracked up to be.

We have all been touched by cancer in some way, and most people will be affected by its awfulness during their lives. That is a terrible, ugly reality. And there's the rub; that a reality can be taken and used and abused as a marketing tool for the furtherment of one person's own image. While this person has no doubt done some good things to help awareness of those affected by the disease, the fact remains that the dreams and hopes proffered were in fact all built on a bed of deception, corruption, lies and fraud. That's not fair to anyone.

Even if you still believe, there are better ways to fight, and better organisations to align your fight with. No one will think you're a better person if you wear a yellow cockring, and it won't prompt them to say to you 'Hey, you fight cancer, that's great' . . . you don't need to tell the world that you are a good person for doing something to help. You can be that person without others telling you so.

RULE #58 //
SUPPORT YOUR LOCAL BIKE SHOP

Never buy bikes, parts or accessories online. Going into your local shop, asking myriad questions, tying up the staff's time, only to go online to buy is akin to having a beer with your best friend before sleeping with his wife. If you do purchase parts online, be prepared to mount and maintain them yourself. If you enter a shop with parts you have bought online and expect them to fit them for you, be prepared to pay handsomely for the shop's time and tip the mechanic.

When we began our journey along the road of La Vie Velominatus, we sought out advice and inspiration from one place: the local bike shop. It was a haven for our kind. We could go there and gaze upon and drool over the latest machines and parts, read magazines about the great feats of extraordinary men in faraway lands and discuss the goings-on in the local racing scene or who had bought that new '10 speed' that came in last week. It was a haven where we felt accepted, where we weren't viewed as outcasts from a society more used to block-headed, no-neck football jocks than weedy Cyclists.

The owner of the shop would usually be an older gentleman, maybe a former top amateur racer in his day, still turning up at the club races and giving it a good go, riding a machine that was top of the line twenty years ago but considered archaic by the young upstarts now. He could still dish out a good dose of The V to them on race day though, and while they would still sneer at his bike, they held him in high regard when it came to his ability to push 30 pounds of steel around the course. While the skin on his face would show the signs of a long life spent on the rivet in the sun and the wind, his legs still looked as though they belonged to a man many decades his junior. Smooth as silk, hard as stone, veins like blood pipes tracking their way to a heart of a horse.

The advent of the internet began to render these doyens of Cycling increasingly rare, to the point of near extinction. New shops were still opening, but run by much younger staff and owned by businessmen who rode as opposed to Cyclists who didn't know much about bookkeeping and audits. The stock changed from racing machines to more generic modes of transport. Cycling, to them, was seen as more of a form of exercise and transport than a passion, or a way of life. To purchase a Campagnolo chain was an exercise in blank looks and inane questions. Online stores exploded across the net, and cheap prices due to low cost overhead meant that the consumer was left with a choice that was easy to make, even if it sat uncomfortably with some of them.

The loyal LBS customer continued to avoid the online stores and frequent their favourite shops. Hanging out at the local shop and being immersed in the local bike culture was every bit as important as buying bikes there. Plus, it was free. Chat rooms were just not the same as having a real, face-to-face argument about the advent of carbon frames or the chances of rain at Paris–Roubaix this spring. We'd see the latest bits and pieces online long before the bike shop could ever get them on their shelves, but being the loyal souls we are, we'd wait until the distributor brought it in and then place an order and pay the retail, less our 'mates rates' discount of course. The part would arrive, we'd get the call, take our bike in, get it fitted for free and ride away happy later that same day. We knew that the parts were properly installed and tuned, but also that if anything did go wrong, the warranty would cover it.

Buying from the internet takes away the experience and knowledge of the hardened mechanics and staff. Punters see 'rear derailleur' at a bargain price and push 'add to cart'. When the part turns up days later and they have no clue as to how to fit it or get it to actually shift across all the cogs, they trudge into the shop and seek out help. When they are told that an 8-speed short-cage derailleur won't work with a 9-speed MTB cassette, they are either sheepish or outright indignant. A reminder to this pitiful few: it's not the shop's fault you don't know your arse from your elbow. Don't get uppity when you're told that you'll need to purchase a new derailleur. And if you happened to get the right one online, don't balk at being told that there'll be a labour charge for your friendly mechanic to fit it. They're not running a charity.

RULE #77 //
RESPECT THE EARTH;
DON'T LITTER

Cycling is not an excuse to litter. Do not throw your empty gel packets, energy bar wrappers or punctured tubes on the road or in the bush. Stuff 'em in your jersey pockets, and repair that tube when you get home.

Cycling and environmentalism are as tied together as celeste and Bianchi. Believe it or not, for every bicycle on earth there are 3.5 stickers equating your car with a forest-clearing, greenhouse-gas-billowing, dolphin-murdering, future-generation-robbing coffin. For this reason, the Keepers don't feel they need to remind you to take care of this place. There are plenty of other self-righteous, sanctimonious assholes doing that already.

What the Keepers do need to remind you of is not to litter the road, countryside or cycleway with the telltale refuse of the Cyclist. We would hope that most Veliminati aren't jackasses and would thus take umbrage with people leaving a trail of shiny foil packets and expended CO_2 canisters in their wake. It can be a long enough rope to push fighting the bad rap we get for wearing Lycra, shaving our legs and thumbing our noses at other Cyclists. If it was easy enough to pull that gel shot from your jersey pocket, it is easy enough to put the empty wrapper back.

RULE #81 //
DON'T TALK IT UP

Rides and crashes may only be discussed and recounted in detail when the rider required external assistance in recovery or recuperation. Otherwise refer to Rule #5.

The oxygen swirling around this small planet is here to fuel your legs; it is not to be wasted talking. Was it raining *really* hard on your last ride? Did you do a *whole* century? Are you *faster* than everyone in your club because of your ceramic hubs? Shut up. Get back on your bike and go ride until you are out of breath and can't talk any more.

La Vie Velominatus is about passion for the ride, the bikes, and the process – not the ego. We talk (and write) of many things, surely, but we do not delude ourselves of greatness undeserved. And should greatness emerge for a fleeting moment, then a stronger rider is surely approaching from behind. Such is the nature of things. Talk is invitation to embarrassment and ridicule; action is salvation. Words will not help when you can't make the bike go. We toil in silence and build strength in our mute suffering ride by ride. When we are the stronger for it, we leave it on the pavement where all who care to know will see it. When we are weaker, we acknowledge and burn harder the next morning.

Talk is a distraction. The pure ride needs no advertisement, no report, no Garmin update. You know what you did and what you did not, so leave it at that. If you would like to revise it, save the talk and get back on the bike tomorrow. We are here for the ride, not the talk.

RULE #89 //
PRONOUNCE IT CORRECTLY

All races shall be referred to by the name given in their country of origin, and care shall be taken to pronounce the name as well as possible. For Belgian races, it is preferable to choose the name given in its region of origin, though it is at the speaker's discretion to use either the Flemish or Wallonian pronunciation. This principle shall also be extended to apply to riders' names, bicycle and component marques and Cycling accoutrements.

American ex-racer and TV personality Bob Roll has abused Rule #89 far too long, and this from a man who can speak Italian. 'The Tour DAAY France' spoken twenty times per hour when covering the race on TV. Was he doing it to drive the multilingual Paul Sherwin mad or to drive us *all* mad? The end result is that it makes Bob Roll sound even less intelligent than he already does. Few who don't reside in Flanders can speak Flemish but at least we can pronounce the Flemish races and locations correctly. Locations, people's names, bike components – all should be pronounced as closely as possible as a speaker of their native language would.

A derailleur is not a de-rail-er.

The *Ronde van Vlaanderen* or *Tour des Flandres* is not the Tour of Flanders.

Super Mario 'Cipo' Cipollini is Cheepo, not a mushroom.

RULE #93 //

DESCENTS ARE NOT FOR RECOVERY. RECOVERY ALES ARE FOR RECOVERY

Descents are meant to be as hard and demanding as – and much more dangerous than – the climbs. Climb hard, descend to close a gap or open one. Descents should hurt, not be a time for recovery. Recovery is designated only for the pub and for shit-talking.

Everyone talks about climbs being hard, but climbing is, in its essence, a simple matter of pushing harder on the pedals. There is an art to it, make no mistake, but going fast uphill comes down to the strength of your will, and with what fury it can make your legs piston the pedals.

Descending, on the other hand, is a matter of either skill or defiance of the imagination.

As one ages, one gets worse at everything except imagining what can go wrong during a high-speed descent. There are two ways to combat this condition: (a) getting better at descending and (b) descending more slowly. Option (b) is not really an option so much as an escape.

Growing up on a bike, I didn't know much about physics, two wheels, tires, or thinking. I just went. The faster, the

better. On one occasion that stands out for the consequences incurred, I dove into a chicane on a descent in
Upstate New York.

We were camping atop the hill, and my brother was staying
in the town down below. We made frequent trips down to
visit him, and I'd learned that all I needed to do to navigate
the bends faster was to pull harder on the bars. On this
particular occasion, I was in hot pursuit of my sister, who
had gotten in front of me. Every boy with an older sister
knows the pressure this put me under, and I had no choice
but to chase her recklessly. Into the turns we went, and I
pulled harder on the bars to accommodate for the speed.
The bicycle, in its stubbornness, kept on its merry way, and
I was forced to disembark. I remember my surprise at how
far I slid. "Like a motorcycle racer," I remember thinking.

Descending is an art form more than any other on the bike.
The forces we play with to stay upright on two wheels are
exaggerated at speed, and cornering only serves to make
things more complicated. There is no sight more beautiful
than a string of riders negotiating a series of bends, the
line making its serpentine way down the mountainside.

There are a few cyclists throughout history who stand out
as masters of descending. Paolo Savoldelli and Philippe
Gilbert are known for the kind of descending that tests the
physics of cornering, causing both tires to slide outward
on the tarmac, at the very limits of their grip.

The Prophet Eddy Merckx was a master of the art. Merckx
could climb; not so much for his size or grace of pedal
stroke, but for his limitless capacity to suffer. But on the
descents, he was in an order altogether apart from his
compatriots. He was known to be a maniac about frame

geometry and his position on the bike; asking his frame builder Ernesto Colnago to build him hundreds of frames, each with marginally differing geometries. He gravitated toward frames that allowed for great stability on the descent, favoring that quality over all else; he knew that if he lost ground to the mountain goats on the climb, his only chance to make up ground would be through finding the fastest way down the other side of the mountain.

In 1971, Merckx found himself more than 8 minutes behind the Spaniard Luis Ocaña on the general classification for the Tour de France. He had been bested on the climbs, but on the Col de Menté, he held his own. To climb the Menté from the east is a challenge already; it climbs, then descends, before finally snaking its brutal way up to the *col*.

The descent, even to think of it now, sends shivers down the spine. It clings loosely to the mountainside; grotesquely exposed, it uses tight switchbacks to wind down toward the valley. By way of safety, low walls of stone line the most exposed bits; walls of the sort of height that do little more than assure you cascade down the mountainside headfirst should you lose control and encounter one.

A fierce thunderstorm swarmed, and as they crested the summit, Merckx plunged down the other side with the dark end of fear and recklessness at his back. Ocaña, in his wake, had too much imagination and crashed in a tight bend. He was then struck by the Dutchman Joop Zoetemelk, who punctured in the same corner and lost control. Ocaña was unable to continue, and Merckx won his third-straight Tour de France.

Fast-forward to 2011 and Andy Schleck, in yellow, suffered a mechanical and was passed by his opponent, Alberto

Contador. Schleck crested the summit 15 seconds behind his adversary with the route heading downhill to the finish. He lost a further 30 seconds, finishing 45 seconds behind the group containing Contador.*

All of which is to say, descents are as much a part of Cycling as the climbs and flats. Learn to ride them, learn to use them to your advantage.

And when it comes to recovery, save it for the ales down at the pub. The harder the ride, the more ales and shit-talking it will take to recover and explain – in ever greater detail – the magnificence of your ride.

*Schleck was later awarded the 2011 Tour after Contador tested positive.

RULE #94 //

USE THE CORRECT TOOL FOR THE JOB, AND USE THE TOOL CORRECTLY

Bicycle maintenance is an art; tools are designed to serve specific purposes, and it is essential that the Velominatus learns to use each tool properly when working on their loyal machine.

I once took to splitting wood with a machete. It worked quite well, for the most part, though the lack of separating action that a splitting axe provides meant that the halves of wood would fly sharply upward, often narrowly missing my head and on one unpleasant occasion, striking it squarely.

I now exclusively use a splitting axe for this purpose, and the result is pleasantly devoid of medical kits and sutures.

A good tool is a work of art – as much an object of function and beauty as our bicycles themselves. It will have a heft to it, telling of the quality of its materials and manufacturing.

Campagnolo is a storied company that knows this about tools; Lezyne is a modern company that knows this about tools. Lezyne makes chain whips and pedal wrenches with wooden handles; the handles absorb grease and dirt and become smooth with use; over time they tell of the journey you've taken together, working on bicycles. All their tools contain a bottle opener; an indication that they understand that bicycles are better worked on with a bottle of ale at the ready.

Campagnolo makes no attempt to hide such extras in their tools, but they do make a wine bottle opener that solves the problem of centering the screw above the cork perfectly. Their tools are as precisely made as their components, each serving a single function sublimely. For some time, they sold complete sets of their tools, all nestled into a sacred case. The first viewing of said case has made earnest men change both their religion and their undergarments. They are not savages, these Italians.

A bicycle is a simple machine, but learning to maintain it is a labor of love; to do so expertly is a skill attained over a lifetime dedicated to the craft. Simple as the machine may be, the tools are specialized gadgets ranging from basic cable cutters and crimpers, to cone wrenches, headset presses and thread taps. Attempting to cut a brake cable with a wire cutter will result in a frayed mess; a cable cutter cuts them perfectly in a single, satisfying snip and keeps the twisted wires in perfect alignment allowing for the installing of a cable end or, if the mechanic is an artisan, soldering.

Screws, nuts and bolts on a good bicycle are made of lightweight alloys that are easily overtightened and stripped. A proper tool will fit precisely and limit any wear or damage. Crescent wrenches are handy for odd sizes, but box end wrenches are much more precise. Use torque wrenches whenever appropriate, and a good sense of mechanics whenever a torque wrench is lacking.

Make investments in the best tools you can afford, and friendships with those who own tools you don't have; a few pints to a mate in exchange for a tool you need to borrow is a pleasure both parties benefit from.

PART II:
The Ride

My lungs feel like they might explode, which is puzzling because I can't seem to get enough air into them. My legs burn to the point of numbness. My head is serving no purpose whatsoever – thinking isn't called for in this instance, no good will come from it – yet it seems so heavy I can hardly hold it up. Even my eyelids and jaw seem weighty; the former want to fall shut and the latter insists on dangling at half past six.

It goes without saying, then, that this is shaping up to be one of my best ever rides.

The Ride is the cathedral of our Craft, where we worship at the altar of the Man with the Hammer and beg to be touched by his seductive spouse, La Volupté. While the Bike may be the central tool of our Craft, to turn the pedals is to experience the sensation of freedom, of flight. Aboard a bicycle, the Cyclist is a graceful creature; on foot, they waddle about like a duckling with a broken leg.

A Cyclist off the bike is just an obnoxious person with shaved legs. When we ride, we are Cyclists. How a Cyclist rides, how a Cyclist becomes one with the bike, it's a little like sex education; there is a lot of misinformation. Rule #59, Hold Your Line – this is not taught in second grade by Miss Scott. Not until one is flying down the road *with another Cyclist* does this become an obvious and important fact of life. Your father is not going to sit you down and give you an awkard and too-brief lecture on Rule #59. And what you hear during recess after Miss Scott's class about bicycle behaviour will just be wrong. The pump goes where? Get outta here!

There are many hallowed rides scattered throughout Europe, where our sport has spent the majority of its developing years. The *cols* of France and the *passi* of Italy are adorned with names that inspire and strike fear in equal measure. Gavia, Stelvio, Galibier, l'Alpe d'Huez and Tourmalet are but a few of the great climbs that every Cyclist should make every reasonable effort to ascend.

The cobblestones of Northern France and West Belgium make up perhaps the most savage roads a bicycle and rider can experience. The Cyclist has no alternative but to ride these roads *à bloc* – full gas. We must learn a new kind of symbiosis as the bicycle jars and rattles over the stones in dissonance with its rider. Every muscle and tendon in the body makes its presence felt as it screams out in desperation. Even the most vivid imagination falls short when picturing what these savage roads are like; the cobbles need to be experienced first hand.

Hallowed ground is one thing, but our world is teeming with amazing roads waiting to be discovered and ridden by the scrupulous Cyclist. With rare exception – usually caused by untenable traffic – every area of the world is filled with mountain and country roads that flow over with possibility.

On the island of Maui in the Hawaiian archipelago lies a volcano called Haleakala. This twisting bit of tarmac is the longest paved road climb on Earth. To ride uphill for 60 kilometres is an experience that is better appreciated from the pub after the ride than it is during the effort itself. Yet, as you stand atop this monster with the knowledge that your legs carried you from sea level to 3,050 metres – over one-third of the height of Mount Everest – you will understand something of the freedom and sense of accomplishment a bicycle can bring in even a relatively short period of time.

This same mountain also holds perhaps the most perfect road for descending. The stretch of road from 1,800 to 1,200 metres passes through vast meadows packed with wide, sweeping hairpin bends. Risk of a catastrophic crash is relatively low and a Cyclist can descend through these corners at speed; the feeling of harmony as you sweep through these bends is so strong that one can hardly contain the urge to whoop and wail in joy.

Blessed are the Cyclists who can ride to work. Starting and ending a workday by laying down a little V makes the working life liveable. Arriving at work slightly blown out and fully awake, having outwitted texting drivers and slippery little hills: this makes the office manageable. The interval between work and home in the evening – it's a chance to let the body burn some energy and the mind to let go the notions of drowning the boss under the water-cooler spigot. When one knows the commute intimately, that short hill past the traffic light, the hipster on their badly tuned fixed-gear bike can be easily dispatched. A victory brought home like the caveman casually dropping a dead warthog at the feet of his wench. Roads everywhere are waiting to be ridden; all we have left to do is set about riding as many as we can manage.

RULE #6 //
FREE YOUR MIND
AND YOUR LEGS WILL
FOLLOW

Your mind is your worst enemy. Do all your thinking before you start riding your bike. Once the pedals start to turn, wrap yourself in the sensations of the ride – the smell of the air, the sound of the tyres, the feeling of flight as the bicycle rolls over the road.

This Rule may have been written backwards, since it is equally true if read in reverse. Granted, it is true enough in either direction. To ride well requires a quiet mind, but the ride itself is the path to enlightenment. One can pedal squares of thought, no less than pedalling squares of the cranks. One can be stuck on an HC climb of the cerebral, too locked on some minutiae of life and work to see the summit within reach.

The solution is to ride, and ride often. Each ride flushes the mind with a fresh dose of all things sensory. The mind opens as the lungs fill. The mind wanders, the legs build power. Ride long enough and the wandering subsides, allowing a clear focus to emerge. This takes practice. Some days it comes easily, on others it will not come at all.

The simplest practice is the daily commute, in whatever

size and shape it takes. To ride every day is to receive the sensory world on its terms: hot, cold, wet, dry – these are all inevitable, and all welcome. Each morning, the day begins with something real, something outside of the mind. Each evening, the mind's new transgressions are brushed back with another immersion in the real, tangible world.

In meditation, the goal is to transcend the physical – to leave the imperfect body behind and attain a higher plane. On the bike, we seek transcendence with the body, not an escape from it. We strive for awareness above discomfort. We aim to be faster, stronger, smoother. We are tuned in, not out. We discipline the body so that we can wrestle the mind, and then – together – take flight.

RULE #20 //

THERE ARE ONLY THREE REMEDIES

FOR PAIN

These are:

- If your quads start to burn, shift forward to use your hamstrings and calves, or
- If your calves or hamstrings start to burn, shift back to use your quads, or
- If you feel weak, meditate on Rule #5 and train more!

Those calves are down there for something other than just intimidation. By engaging the ankle, hamstrings and calves one can take some pressure off the quads. The quads may help mash the pedals from one o'clock to four o'clock but the calves and some supple ankles will continue power transmission through the seven o'clock position. The hamstrings will be engaged on the upstroke to bring the pedal up to eleven o'clock where the calves and ankles again finish the job to bring it back round to one o'clock.

Options one and two are useful for about thirty seconds and then it's on to remedy three. Rule #5 is how a Cyclist ultimately deals with pain. Pain is good. Pain is fleeting.

There are many faces to pain. Pain should be the friend that one invites over now and again. Invite pain in, offer tea, pain refuses, one asks pain to leave and come back another day. It is an indicator that you are alive and attempting to lay down some V. It may also mean one is going into the red zone and the great slowing is about to happen.

Training *is* Cycling; if you don't like training, you don't like Cycling. Even for the non-racer (most everyone), training is just as important. One is still racing against that old git and his wife on mountain bikes you just barely passed. That wiry kid in cut-off jeans and sneakers coming up behind you on the long hill, it's *On like Donkey Kong*! We may all be racing against grim death but that kid is Death with a rusty, creaky chain. If he catches you, you are fucked.

Every dodge gained over years of riding must be used: if all else fails and Death in denim cut-offs is still gaining, it's Rule #5, bitches. Shift up, heave out of the saddle and make like Stephen Roche pulling back time on Pedro Delgado in the '87 Tour de France. That kid is not going to catch you, even if he has been abusing amyl nitrates all the way from Grandma's house. You go until that kid is broken, open up a gap so huge he can't hear your animal bleats and pleas to the Madonna as you move Sur la Plaque over the top of said hill and disappear away, Il Falcone, descending to either hide behind a hedge or duck into a pub.

That is why one trains. The race may come to you when you least expect it, and you had better be ready.

RULE #38 //
DON'T PLAY LEAP FROG

Train Properly: if you get passed by someone, it is nothing personal; just accept that on the day/effort/ride they were stronger than you. If you can't deal, work harder. But don't go playing leapfrog to get in front only to be taken over again (multiple times) because you can't keep up the pace. Especially don't do this just because the person overtaking you is a woman. Seriously. Get over it.

There seems to be a subset of riders out there who take it way too personally should they be passed by another, faster rider or group. Maybe they had older siblings growing up who would always win the race to the letterbox, who would pinch their ice cream cone from them and never wait when they went riding their bikes down to the old quarry. And they've never gotten over it.

It seems that these poor sods were also predetermined to wear YJAs and ride mountain bikes with dry, squeaky chains to their office jobs. The Commuter Grand Prix can be a harsh and dangerous place, mainly because the levels of competitiveness are exaggerated way beyond a simple bike ride to get to work, and elevated to the same status as getting promoted from junior accountant to senior accountant that day – they just *have* to be there as early as possible so that Wilson from the third floor doesn't get in there and brown-nose his way in first. Here comes Wilson up the hall, he's passing my desk, better head him off at the photocopier. Take that, Wilson.

Natural selection usually sorts this whole mess out, but sometimes the selection process can be a hard taskmaster, so best be careful. Recently our small group climbed a known-to-be-busy, narrow road behind a lone mountain-biker. We respected our own, his and surrounding motorists' safety and convenience by staying behind him until the top where we had sufficient room to pass. Not long after we'd passed and bid our greetings to him, we were forced to stop behind a row of stationary traffic at a major intersec-tion. No sooner had we casually draped ourselves on our top tubes than Old Mate Mountain Bike rattled past not only us, and not only the six or so idling cars sat going nowhere, but did this all while on the wrong side of the road with oncoming traffic approaching. A collective disbe-lieving, nervous chuckle rippled through our group, but no one would have been laughing had a collision ensued.

Of course, we caught up to him about twenty metres up the road, and were again stuck behind him, an unnecessary eventuality of his fatuous, childishly inconsiderate determi-nation to get ahead again. We re-passed him, never to be seen again. Maybe he learned a little about himself that day, but probably not. But we certainly did.

RULE #39 //
NEVER RIDE WITHOUT
YOUR EYEWEAR

You should not make a habit of riding without eyewear, although approved extenuating circumstances include fog, overheating and low-light conditions. When not worn over the eyes, they should be neatly tucked into the vents of your helmet. If they don't fit, buy a new helmet. In the meantime you can wear them backwards on the back of your head or carefully tuck them into your jersey pocket, making sure not to scratch them on your tools (see Rule #31).

Phil Anderson drops his competitors with the help of his Oakley Factory Pilots.

There are no two ways about it: we live in a three-dimensional world and the principal mechanism we rely on to navigate it without bumping into things all day long is our sense of sight. Sight seems a simple thing, and it's something we routinely take for granted, despite the mind-blowingly complex mathematics involved in determining the precise distance an obstacle is from us and making navigational recommendations to our brain to guide our various append-ages to help us avoid (or allow us to hit) whatever it is they've spotted.

The only thing that rivals our eyeballs' innate awesomeness, though, is their fragility. I have observed that it is rather unpleasant when our eyes are fooled about with. A bit of dust or an eyelash gone astray and I'm in a heap on the floor trying my best to regain both my vision and composure. When I was a teenager, I got a smack in the face that cracked my skull from the eye socket to the jawbone and that made one of my eyeballs sway to the side for a month or so while my face healed. It was incredibly unpleasant, partly because it hurt but mostly because my brain couldn't cope with one of my eyes being on spring break while the other was trying to do half the trigonometry and so forth that we rely on not to fall over. The result was a severe headache and a protracted period of bumping into rather a lot of things. As my mum says, I was half a metre left of centre.

The fact is not lost on me that when we set out on our bicycles we invite dust, rocks, rain and small mammals to fly into our ocular receptacles. I use the phrase 'ocular receptacle' because it's the term that makes this sound like the biggest, hairiest deal possible, because that's precisely what losing the use of our eyes is.

It wasn't until the mid-eighties that Cycling-specific eyewear came available. Until then we depended on the small brim of the Cycling cap to shield our eyes from those things a Cyclist encounters that can blind us. The Cycling cap had until that time dispatched its short visor to keep the elements at bay, as well as by providing a bit of shade and forming a small draught just below the brim that would discourage dust and debris from flying into our eyes.

That isn't to say there hasn't been some exploration into alternatives. In the 20s and 30s, riders made use of motor-cycle goggles to keep gravel and grit out of the eyes. There is little evidence that the goggles did more than sit atop their foreheads and look Cool because, as it turns out, riding a bicycle is quite a lot of work and a foam-lined goggle is prone to fogging up during exertion– and fog impedes the primary function of the eyes.

The answer to the question of who pioneered the modern Cycling-specific eyewear is divided cleanly betwixt hemi-spheres. In the Northern Hemisphere, we believe this pioneer to be Greg 'LeMan' LeMond. In the Southern Hemisphere, it is largely held to be Phil Anderson. Since history is written by the victor and only one of those riders won the Tour de France, the Northern Hemisphere will tell you they pioneered Cycling-specific eyewear and they would be right. But, since the Southern Hemisphere carries a hefty chip upon their shoulder, they will tell you the same. We may never know which side is right, mostly because the Australians can't stay sober long enough to finish the argument.

In the mid-eighties, Oakley adapted their ski goggles to the Cycling world, modifying their design to be more lightweight and to utilise an earpiece instead of an elastic headband to keep them in place.

Greg LeMond, Andy Hampsten, Phil Anderson and several other visionaries immediately recognised the benefit of being able to see while riding a bike and adopted them for use in the peloton. Their sudden popularity in the bunch mirrored that of clipless pedals and within a few years there were only a few hold-outs who refused to embrace their utility.

Today, Cycling-specific eyewear protects us from wind, rain, dust, debris and even differing degrees of sunlight, as recent technology has introduced effective photosensitive sunglasses. If you're rolling in a pair of blue-blockers or Ray-Bans, ditch them immediately and pick up a pair of proper, Cycling-specific sunglasses.

RULE #42 //
A BIKE RACE SHALL NEVER BE PRECEDED WITH A SWIM AND/OR FOLLOWED BY A RUN

If it's proceeded with a swim and/or followed by a run, it is not called a bike race, it is called a duathlon or a triathlon. Neither of which is a bike race. Also keep in mind that one should only swim in order to prevent drowning and should only run if being chased. And even then, one should only run fast enough to prevent capture.

It is probably just as difficult to resist lambasting tri-hards as it is for the reader to realise that we are, in fact, not lambasting them. Well, maybe we are – just a little. But this Rule speaks more to the tradition and culture of road Cycling and road racing in particular.

We'll take a look at the essence of road racing first as it is quite simple. A bike race is called a bike race because one races bikes in the event and nothing else. Long before someone got the idea to wedge a bike ride in between a swim and a run, people were starting and finishing races on bicycles. The task was to establish which rider was the fastest as they rode from somewhere to somewhere else. If there was any running involved it was for the necessity of either push-starting the team leader back up to speed after giving him your bike due to a mechanical problem, or possibly dismounting to run short distances over barriers or other obstacles during a cyclocross race. In either case, the point of running is not for the sake of running, but to get back to Cycling as soon as possible.

As far as swimming is concerned, well, it is much harder to discern why anybody ever thought swimming in conjunction with Cycling would be a worthwhile pursuit. Swimming is a leisure activity that takes place in the summer (or at a pre-season training camp in a tropical locale resulting in embarrassing photo-ops with teammates), at a beach, and typically involves a cooler of malted beverages. It is certainly always accompanied by the fear of blending one's crisp tan lines cultivated in Cycling kit and for this reason alone it should be avoided.

There is also a tradition in road racing that Rule #42 addresses. Rule #42 at once speaks to the Disciple's need to adhere to Rule #10 and gives her a perfectly legitimate excuse to be lazy off the bike. It is well known that pro Cyclists will do whatever it takes to do absolutely nothing while they are not training or racing. Stories abound in the peloton of riders couch-surfing for hours on end during rest days. George Hincapie was known to be a couch-surfing Sensei, watching the telly while everything he needed to eat and communicate with the outside world was only an arm's reach away. It has also been said that Coppi and Hinault both went as far as to have their *soigneurs* carry them up flights of stairs in their hotels during Grand Tours to conserve energy for the next day. Do you think it even crossed their minds to go for a jog or have a swim to unwind after a bike race? These men were concerned with one thing and one thing only: riding their bikes batshit fast.

RULE #49 //
KEEP THE RUBBER
SIDE DOWN

It is completely unacceptable to intentionally turn one's steed upside down for any reason under any circumstances. Besides the risk of scratching the saddle, levers and stem, it is unprofessional and a disgrace to your loyal steed. The risk of the bike falling over is increased, wheel removal/replacement is made more difficult and your bidons will leak. The only reason a bicycle should ever be in an upside-down position is during mid-rotation while crashing. This Rule also applies to upside-down saddle-mount roof bars.

If one sees a rider in distress, his bike upside down, his chain hopelessly tangled with his frame and cassette, don't stop. Look at him with a pitiless gaze, as if to ask, 'What the fuck are you doing, you tosser, learn how to remove a wheel and then I'll help you.' And still keep riding by.

Helping our fellow Cyclists-in-need is an obligation of the Velominati, but we have our limits. Giving up our only inner tube, offering the four-minute master class in fixing a flat tyre roadside, tightening a slipping seat post, these are all services one should willingly bestow on a fellow rider.

Enabling the bike flipper by assisting him does not help him. Showing a bike flipper how to untangle his upside-down

This is acceptable.

chain is useless (and you will get chain lube on your hands).
Teach him to not flip his bike so the chain never gets tangled
in the first place; that is a lesson worth teaching.

The Ancient Velomis Proverb states: *Show a Cyclist how to
accomplish roadside repairs on his machine in the proper
position and you still may get grease on your hands. Teach
him to do it himself, and your hands will stay clean.*

Do you ever see a professional flip his bike upside down while waiting for the team car to bring up the mechanic? Do car mechanics flip a car to work on it? A veterinarian a horse? Nay.

As Gentullio 'Tullio' Campagnolo raced up the freezing cold Croce D'Aune Pass in 1927, he paused to change gears. Changing gears meant removing the rear wheel, turning it round to access the second cog on the other side of the hub and refixing the wheel in the frame . . . good times. Naturally, the aluminium wing nuts holding the rear wheel in the frame were properly iced over and frozen solid. Tullio was unable to change gears. There was much questioning the Madonna's purity on the flanks of the Croce D'Aune that day. There was also no flipping of the steed over in the snow while this was going on. Thank Merckx he couldn't loosen those wing nuts, because it led to him to develop many things we take for granted on the modern bicycle, including the quick-release skewer and the gear derailleur. He didn't flip out when faced with a mechanical, and nor should you.

RULE #55 //
EARN YOUR
TURNS

If you are riding down a mountain, you must first have ridden up the mountain. It is forbidden to employ powered transportation simply for the cheap thrill of descending. The only exception to this is if you are doing intervals on Alpe d'Huez or the Plan de Corones and you park your car up top before doing twenty repeats of the climb.

Frank labours up Haleakala in Hawaii as tourists hire bikes to ride down. Disgraceful.

If a mountain is worth riding down it is most certainly worth riding up. This is yet another distinction between the Cyclist and a bicycle rider. The Cycling Disciple seeks out pain and a beautiful effort on the bike. When we see a 12-per-cent grade punctuated by 18-per-cent switchbacks we point our front wheel toward it and revel in the suffering. When we reach the summit we may or may not stop for a drink before speeding to the valley below as our legs sigh in relief before the start of the next climb and the lactic-acid bath that will surely accompany it. It is of no concern whether we are built like a Schleck or can dance on the pedals like Charly Gaul. What does matter is that we yearn for passes to come and pine for the *cols* we have left behind. When asked how his ride up Luz Ardiden went, the Velominatus should reply, 'I suffered like I've never suffered before. It was fantastic.'

RULE #59 //
HOLD YOUR LINE

Ride predictably, don't make sudden movements. Under no circumstances are you to deviate from your line.

Much of what is outlined in this sacred text can be considered to be equal parts style, tradition, function and tongue planted firmly in cheek. To be clear, you *will* align your tyre label over your valve stem and you will *not* use a European Posterior Man-Satchel. But if for some strange reason you choose to disobey these edicts, the consequences wouldn't amount to more than a belittling reminder from another Velominatus or perhaps a few lashes with a mini-pump. Rule #59, however, needs to be taken seriously and with a healthy dose of respect because non-adherence to this particular Rule can be disastrous for both rider and bike.

In order to fully grasp the concept of holding one's line, the Disciple must understand that riding a bicycle in a large pack – be it during a race or a group ride – is not an entirely individual endeavour. Cycling in a bunch requires just enough humility to recognise that what is good for the goose is good for the gander. Nothing will get you uninvited from the local club ride quicker than riding erratically, half-wheeling and generally being unpredictable on the bike. Holding your position in a group takes practice but it's the only way you're going to get to the pointy end of the group and stay there – and it's most often how you'll get yourself in the position to cross the finish line first.

You can also refer to this Rule on your solo training rides, as it's in your own best interests to remain consistent and predictable to motorists and pedestrians. Follow the logical lines of the road and signal your intentions when turning or stopping and, if you can, when making any drastic course changes. You are, after all, a nearly naked person on eight kilos of vehicle, dancing with cars piloted by teenagers too young and geriatrics too old. Give them all the help you can.

RULE #63 //
POINT IN THE DIRECTION
YOU'RE TURNING

Signal a left turn by pointing your left arm to the left. To signal a right turn, simply point with your right arm to the right. This one is, presumably, mostly for Americans: that right-turn signal that Americans are taught to make with your left arm elbow-out and your forearm pointing upwards was developed for motor vehicles prior to the invention of the electric turn signal since it was rather difficult to reach from the driver-side all the way out the passenger-side window to signal a right turn. On a bicycle, however, we don't have this limitation and it is actually quite easy to point your right arm in the direction you are turning.

American bicyclists have two idiotic inclinations. The first is to ride on the wrong side of the road, against traffic. We were taught to do this, I presume, in an effort to curb overpopulation brought on by the baby boom. Aside from some measure of guilt on the part of the driver who dispatches bicycles moving in the wrong direction over the hood of their car, it is a much tidier approach to culling the population than a stealth artillery operation is because you simply can't coordinate the offensive effectively and people always ask questions afterwards.

The other is the tendency to signal a right turn by pointing at the sky. Visit any bicycle-friendly city across the country and you will find a myriad of riders wobbling about as they approach an intersection, pointing to the heavens. Exactly what they are pointing to, I'm not clear, but it certainly doesn't look like a right turn.

On the other hand, pointing in the direction we are turning (left to turn left, and right to turn right) has the dual benefit of being clear and of being universally understood across the world, by any driver, whether traffic moves on the right side of the road – or the wrong side.

A final point of consideration is that while we must always be clear in signalling the turn, we must remain Casually Deliberate at all times; approaching a corner, I find it a good practice to signal once well before the turn and a second time just before I grip the bars and lean into the corner.

RULE #64 //
CORNERING CONFIDENCE INCREASES WITH TIME AND EXPERIENCE

This pattern continues until it falls sharply and suddenly.

Let us address this Rule in its two parts. It is instructive to watch motorcycle-racing deity Valentino Rossi go through wet corners at 130 miles per hour. He has confidence and experience. The only three advantages he holds over a Cyclist are a larger contact patch of rubber on the road, more expensive rubber compounds in his tyres and a motorcycle's suspension holding the tyres to the track. Wearing full leathers as opposed to some skintight Lycra could be considered a fourth advantage but that depends on how much you like Lycra and road rash.

Happily, Michelin makes both bicycle tyres and Rossi's tyres, so we get to enjoy the benefit of their motorcycle-racing experience. Also in our favour: Valentino and his Ducati weigh much more than our bicycles and us so the forces of destruction are much greater for him. What keeps us from greater cornering confidence is a healthy distrust in our tyres' ability to grip the road, especially wet roads.

Following a rider who is better at cornering than you is the best way to improve. Follow their line and notice how little they brake as they approach the corner. If they are good, their hands are nowhere near the brake levers. They trust their tyres. They trust them because they did not spend as little money as possible on them. The salesperson who touts a tyre that will last a lifetime is the one who should be going over the guardrail, not you. Motorcycle race tyres barely last one race! Bike tyres should not be constructed of so hard a rubber compound that they last for more than 10,000km. You gave your tyres a quick inspection before leaving for your ride, didn't you? Like the pilots you see through your aeroplane window, madly kicking the jet's tyres and tugging on the flaps during their preflight check, before take-off is the time to notice the slit in your front tyre. Noticing it as you eject from your two-wheeled cockpit and attempt a Lycra landing on the tarmac is not a good time for it.

Ride top-quality tyres at a proper inflation pressure. Professional Cyclists ride tyres inflated to very high pressures, often higher than optimum. It is another long-held tradition that very hard tyres are faster. They might feel faster as you rattle along the road but this has been shown to not always be true, especially in cornering. The higher the pressure, the smaller the contact patch is with the road and the less the sidewall of the tyre can deflect to keep that contact patch on the road.

Finally, do *not* think about the second half of this Rule, that bit about your confidence dropping sharply and suddenly. This is true, of course; after a crash, it takes some time to regain the trust that you once had in your tyres. The trust that is lost is directly proportional to how surprising the crash was. If you feel it coming, a little bit at a time, that is one thing. If you slip on some black ice mid-corner – going from perfectly fine to a heap in the ditch in the space of an instant – that is another thing altogether.

But thinking of this does no good. Think about good things. Think about where it is you want to go. Think about how good it feels as you take the perfect line through a corner. Or don't think at all. If ever there is a time for human and machine to be one it is here.

RULE #67 //
DO YOUR TIME IN
THE WIND

Nobody likes a wheel-sucker. You might think you're playing a smart tactical game by letting everyone else do the work while you sit on, but races (even Town Sign Sprints) are won through cooperation and spending time on the rivet, flogging yourself and taking risks. Riding wheels and jumping past at the end is one thing and one thing only: poor sportsmanship.

Many years ago, I decided that my Cycling was at a point where I needed to 'train'. Riding just didn't seem to be the thing to do any more; I was racing every weekend, and of course racing means training. Every ride had to produce some results, some tangible benefit that would help me to be beaten by other, more dedicated racers by a little bit less each time. So I signed up for a ten-day 'training tour' around a small island outpost somewhere south of civilisation. It felt like the thing to do, my own little slice of Mallorca or Mexico.

There was a good mix of riders on the tour, not what I'd expected in terms of the young and the hungry riders, but older, yet still hungry (and thirsty) sea dogs. We ate and drank a lot that week. The nature of the riding was more Audax than stage race, but it was more fun than any structured heart-rate fest would have been. We were competitive, but rode largely together for most of the time most of the days. We helped each other when we were suffering, and we shared the workload and time in the wind so we could make it to the buffet and bar with something in reserve to deal with digestion of food and consumption of beer.

Except one guy.

At first it wasn't much more than a bit of a laugh at his expense. The light-hearted digs about his hair not being out of place from lack of wind, the cute little nicknames like 'Wheel Magnet' seemingly taken with a good dose of humour. As the week wore on and bodies and minds wore down from the long days in the hot sun and dry wind, tolerance gave way to temper. This limpet had latched on to one wheel too many, and every attempt to manoeuvre him to the front was somehow foiled by his cunning positioning and under-handed tactics. There was no way this guy was going to the front, so it was decided he must then go out the back. Attacks were predetermined en masse, and carried out ad nauseum until he would curl up and drop off the last survivor like a salted leech. We didn't care that our Neanderthal tactics were conspiring only to wear ourselves out at a greater rate than we could reasonably afford; we'd tried the civilised way and our limits of compassion and tact had well and truly been reached. The penny dropped for 'The Magnet' after a day or two of eating alone as well, and lo and behold, who should pop up at the front for the remainder of the trip!

A valuable lesson had been learned, a new term had entered our lexicon (wheel magnet) and all was right with the world. Until the following year's tour . . .

RULE #68 //
RIDES ARE TO BE MEASURED BY QUALITY
NOT QUANTITY

Rides are to be measured by the quality of their distance and never by distance alone. For climbing rides, distances should be referred to by the amount of vertical covered; flat and rolling rides should be referred to by their distance and average speed. For example, declaring 'We rode 4km' would assert that 4000m were climbed during the ride, with the distance being irrelevant. Conversely, a flat ride of 150km at 23kmh is not something that should be discussed in an open forum and Rule #5 must be reviewed at once.

If you have ever ridden a single secteur of pavé in the Nord Pas de Calais or a cobbled berg near Oudenaarde, you have lived – and therefore understand – this Rule. One passage through the Trouée d'Arenberg or up the Koppenberg is roughly equivalent to the totality of your best season of riding the monotonous roads near your home. It is a religious experience akin to that of any believer making the most holy of pilgrimages.

The reason for this has as much to do with the type of riding these places offer as much as it does with their historical significance to Cycling. Paris–Roubaix is typically a 260-kilometre race but the initial 100 kilometres to the

The Koppenberg rises to the heavens.

first pavé secteur are ridden virtually neutralised, but for the occasional hopeless breakaway.

The racers know that it is only the last 150km, and particularly the 50km of cobbled roads spread out over some twenty-seven or twenty-eight secteurs, that matters. These roads have a puzzling way of at once depleting and energising you. They make themselves apparent under your tyre by punishing every bone, joint and muscle in your body. It is a small miracle that your bike doesn't fold beneath you as it skips roughly in a straight line down the crown of the cobbled road.

Throughout the controlled chaos involving rider, machine and stone you are strangely motivated to squeeze every last bit of strength from your legs as you struggle to maintain speed and stay upright. Every neuron in your brain is focussed on the fact that the road is doing everything it can to stop you from progressing. To the Cycling Disciple, this is as good as riding gets. The riding here is of such quality that it matters not that you just rode 260 kilometres for the day. What matters is that you took each secteur in the moment and pushed hard against every last cobblestone that banged your wheels back against your body. The total is much larger than the sum of the parts.

When traversing the considerably less demanding and exciting roads of their local ride, the Cycling Disciple must

Not all rides can be on the hallowed Pavé du Nord.

be mindful of the fact that they will never approximate the level of Awesome held by the hallowed roads of the sport. What the Disciple can do, however, is approach each ride with the attitude that within any given ride of any given length there are myriad ways to improve the quality of the ride. Focus on the breath, push a larger gear, centre in on your V-Locus, endeavour to meet The Man with the Hammer. Pursuing any of these within a 100 km ride is much more noble than putting an easy 200 km behind you. Make no mistake; both are kilometres in the V-Bank. Only one, however, trades in the currency of the Velominatus.

RULE #79 //
FIGHT FOR YOUR TOWN LINES

Town lines must be contested or at least faked if you're not into it or too shagged to do anything but pedal the bike.

In the US of A even sleepy secondary roads have a posted marking when moving across from one town into another. The signage is often subtle and never foretold. It's the opposite of the Tour de France's green jersey sprint line where its arrival is marked in approaching kilometres and finally metres. The town line becomes the green jersey's sprint line but these sprints are unannounced and unnoticed to anyone but the riders leaving one town and entering another. Bike racing is a tactical sport. It's not the strongest who always wins. Small group finishes are little chess games. Developing a sprint is training. Developing your sprint with your abilities takes practice. Training has to be enjoyed. As an amateur, there is a one hundred percent chance you don't have a lead-out train. So you have to finish on your own strengths and wits. Rule #79 is here to help.

If your guns are entirely devoid of fast twitch muscles you can still win a sprint finish but it takes practice. It is a trick of alchemy to do it: timing, head games, bluffing and maybe some luck, but it happens all the time. If you have some fast twitch muscles, you may find that after 160km they don't twitch so much and still anything is possible. If you are the fastest finisher in a group, everyone knows it and you still have to be brilliant to win. Even being brilliant takes practice and racing for town lines is a perfect way to learn. It also breaks up the monotony of a long group-training ride. Trash-talking makes for amusing kilometres. One gets the experience of recovering from a sprint effort and not getting dropped 60km from home.

Nervously changing gears as a town line approaches alerts those who are listening; dropping back in the group does too. Who even knows where the town line is? Who even remembers about town lines 120km into a group ride? Who has any juice left? Who is even interested in sprinting? Who just wants to get home with the group? Who is messing with their shifters with zero intention of sprinting, just to screw with the more ambitious sprinters' heads?

It may not be racing but it is fun and an effective use of your training time.

RULE #83 //
BE SELF-SUFFICIENT

Unless you are followed by a team car, you will repair your own punctures and mechanicals, should you encounter any. You will do so expediently, employing your own skills, using your own equipment and without complaining that your expensive tyres are too tight for your puny thumbs to fit over your expensive rim. The fate of a rider who has failed to equip himself pursuant to Rule #31, or who knows not how to use said equipment, shall be determined at the discretion of any accompanying or approaching rider in accordance with Rule #84.

The Bike is the central tool in our Craft and it is paramount that it be properly maintained and cared for. At first, it seems a terribly complicated thing to understand; the pushing and pulling of cables and chains over cogs with chain wheels that somehow manage to bring the contraption into motion. Properly tuned, a bicycle in flight makes almost no noise at all; only the whistle of the tyres can be heard as rider and machine engage in their harmonious flight together.

One of the great pleasures in this sport is learning how to expertly care for our beloved machine: to tune the shifting, true a wheel or adjust the brakes. To learn to care for and maintain the bicycle is to become more closely bonded with this device from which we derive such pleasure. Looking after it properly strengthens the bond between man and machine.

There is also a critical safety consideration; a well-maintained bicycle is a safe bicycle. When left in disrepair, the machine becomes unreliable; a mechanical failure is a cruel thing to encounter at high speed.

In the care of the diligent Velominatus, the bicycle is routinely checked over and critical items checked prior to each ride. This greatly reduces the quantity of roadside repairs that will be required while out on a ride, though it is folly to presume no such incident will occur.

Therefore, the Cyclist must always carry with them the tools they will require in order to mend any problem they might encounter: a mini-tool, spare tubes and inflation device are the minimum equipment required.

Hope is not a strategy against mishaps; be prepared with the supplies and knowledge you need in order to return home safely from your ride.

RULE #84 //
FOLLOW THE CODE

Consistently with The Code Of The Domestique, the announcement of a flat tyre in a training ride entitles – but does not oblige – all riders then present in the bunch to cease riding without fear of being labeled Pussies. All stopped riders are thereupon entitled – but not obliged – to lend assistance, instruction and/or stringent criticism of the tyre-mender's technique. The duration of a Rule #84 stop is entirely discretionary, but is generally inversely proportional to the duration of the remaining time available for post-ride espresso.

Place five Cyclists at the roadside with a flat tyre and you will hear at least five different ways to mend it. What position to place the lever at in order to most effectively remove the tyre – or whether to use a lever at all. How best to remove the tube and locate the puncture. Whether to use CO_2 or pump. What angle to hold the pump, whether to replace the wheel prior to or after inflating. To what pressure to inflate them, whether to include talc powder: the list goes on.

The remarkable thing about this isn't the myriad of puncture-repair possibilities in how to mend a puncture, but rather the Cyclist's totalistic inability to keep their advice to themselves until asked. Instead, the five will stand in a semicircle around the poor bloke doing the mending and simultaneously bombard him with their cherished nuggets of advice. Given the fact that they will be speaking in unison, the customary reaction is to increase the volume of their own advice. This, in turn, results in a near-simultaneous escalation of volume until the entire group is reduced to a troop of skinny, Lycra-clad howler monkeys.

On a long ride this past summer, a fellow rider suffered a puncture during the opening kilometres of our ride. Knowing we had a long day ahead of us, I urged the group to continue on while I waited with him as he fixed his flat. I didn't want the group to wait and I also knew it would be difficult for him to bridge back up alone. A rider with whom to share the work would be a welcome asset, I reasoned.

He expertly removed his back wheel and set about removing the tyre. Within moments, he had broken a lever in his vain attempt to dislodge the stubborn thing. After an epic struggle, he finally managed to free it from the rim and set about mending the leaking tube.

His attempts to reseat the tyre were a typical blend of comic ingenuity and unrelenting frustration; just as the tyre was about to snap onto the rim at one end, it would wiggle free at the other. I felt like I was watching an M.C. Escher drawing unfold in real time.

In the end, the task required both our hands and more than a few curses to get the tyre on and to find ourselves back on the road. Given the length of the struggle, by the time we succeeded, we had quite a chase ahead of us.

Very kind of him, then, to drop me on the first climb so I might struggle back to the group alone.

RULE #85 //
DESCEND LIKE A PRO

All descents shall be undertaken at speeds commonly regarded as 'ludicrous' or 'insane' by those less talented. In addition all corners will be traversed in an outside-inside-outside trajectory, with the outer leg extended and the inner leg canted appropriately (but not so far as to replicate a motorcycle racer, for you are not one), to assist in balance and creation of an appealing aesthetic. Brakes are generally not to be employed, but if absolutely necessary, only just prior to the corner. Also see Rule #64.

This is a tall order because the majority of pros descend like demons. Any idiot can point their bike down the mountain and drop like a stone, but it is the first corner that distinguishes the competent descender from the idiot who just went over the guardrail. It is an evil cocktail of experience, bravado and necessity that professionals guzzle in huge quantities that allows them to descend into corners faster than their TV motorcycles can. The rest of us can still descend like pros but maybe not as fast. Pros also crash and we all like to avoid that.

There are a few skills to master that will make descending more fun, faster and involve fewer trips to the bathtub for sessions scrubbing the grit out of dermal abrasions.

The first is setting up for the corner by putting the bike to the outside of the road approaching the corner. Even if the road is multiple S-turns, it's imperative one gets to the outside edge of the road so one can head for the apex (inside) of the corner and continue to the outside to exit the corner. In a 90-degree corner the radius doubles when taken outside, inside, outside. The larger the radius, the faster one can ride through it.

Braking and cornering do not mix. Consult your local nerdy physics major for an exciting lecture that is guaranteed to include the words gyroscope, gyroscopic, steering axis, tilting forces and possibly, if lucky, angular deceleration. The take-home message is this: when leaned over in a turn and brakes are strongly applied, the bike will stand up and track straight. That is not good. We then enter a bad feedback loop between a bike that is going straight when it should be cornering and additional force on the brake lever. It never ends well.

One also hopes to lower one's centre of gravity, getting it down low near those road-gripping tyres. Pressing down on the outside pedal is wise. Bending the elbows to lower the torso is too.

In summary:
- Set up to the outside before sweeping in towards the inside apex corner.
- Do your braking before starting to corner, then get the hell off those brake levers.
- Get your centre of gravity low.
- Stay loose and supple.

RULE #86 //
DON'T HALF-WHEEL

Never half-wheel your riding partners; it's terrible form – it is always the other guy who sets the pace. Unless, of course, you are on the rivet, in which case it's an excellent intimidation technique.

I have to admit, I'm a half-wheeler. I do it habitually, even though I really mean no disrespect by it. In fact, it's quite the opposite; I'm actually trying to be polite.

You see, I was always taught to look people in the eye when I'm speaking to them. Cycling side by side prohibits this almost entirely, so I instinctively roll forward just enough that I can turn my head back and see the person's face while we're having our little chat.

In truth, half-wheeling is perhaps the most passive-aggressive behavior anyone can undertake on a bicycle. One rider moves their wheel forward and the other rider responds by matching it. Up and up the pace goes, until both riders are going flat-out, hammering away like idiots. What started out as an 'easy ride' has now turned into a hammerfest and any notion of Training Properly has been abolished to the darkness of pointless competition.

On the other hand, the half-wheel is possibly the most devastating tool to wield during a psychological battle.

Hungry for a draught, riders normally ride behind one another, grateful for the wind shadow provided by the wheel in front. But not always.

During the 1964 Tour de France, Jacques Anquetil wore the yellow jersey ahead of his countryman Raymond Poulidor. Poulidor was the better climber, Anquetil the better strategist. As the race went up the final climb to the Puy de Dôme, Anquetil knew he would be outmatched by Poulidor. But instead of marking him or going on the attack, Jacques employed a masterful tactic: he simply rode alongside Raymond.

Up and up they went, one beside the other, matched pedal stroke for pedal stroke. How Anquetil must have suffered that day, how Poulidor must have been tortured to see his rival match his every stroke.

Near the top of the climb, Poulidor finally escaped Anquetil's grip, but it was too late to do enough damage to win the race. Anquetil rode into Paris as victor for the fifth and final time.

**Anquetil half-wheels Poulidor into the ground
on the Puy du Dome.**

RULE #87 //
THE RIDE STARTS ON TIME.
NO EXCEPTIONS

The upside of always leaving on time is considerable. Others will be late exactly once. You signal that the sanctity of this ride, like all rides, is not something with which you should muck. You demonstrate, not with words but with actions, your commitment. As a bonus, you make more time for post-ride espresso. 'On Time', of course, is taken to mean at V past the hour or half hour.

You spend a lot of time mentally and physically preparing to ride. You daydream about your bike, staring through your significant other as their mouth moves, apparently saying something. Your employer's bandwidth is used for one part filing TPS reports and three parts Cycling websites. Your kids wouldn't be going to that second-rate public university were it not for that last hand-laid carbon bike you hid at your mate's place until it cools off enough to bring home and claim as merely 'that old thing'. Suffice it to say, adherence to the Rules #1–#86 has led you here, to Rule #87, the ride itself. So why, in Merckx's name, would you waste time by starting it late?

Pedro Delgado, the Patron Saint of Rule #87, would have most certainly had a very different Tour in 1989 had he not shown up to the prologue 2 minutes and 40 seconds late. Wearing the *Maillot Jaune* of the defending champion, Delgado rode a strong prologue in Luxembourg that year, just seven weeks after his victory in the Vuelta. In fact, Perico, as he was known, had at least as much, if not more, of a chance than his two greatest rivals, Laurent Fignon and Greg LeMond, of winning. But he started his ride late, and that was a hefty price to pay.

Delgado fought back and arguably gave the performance of his life, ultimately landing on the third step of the podium in Paris. His final deficit to the winners (Lemond and Fignon respectively) was more than the 2:40 he lost in the prologue but we'll never know what could have been and one can imagine it took Perico a while to get over Delgado'ing the Prologue in the '89 Tour.

Delgado is a Giant of the Road but, unfortunately, largely remembered by some for showing up late to La Grande Boucle.

RULE #88 //
DON'T SURGE

When rolling onto the front to take your turn in the wind – see Rule #67 – do not suddenly lift the pace unless trying to establish a break. The key to maintaining a high average speed is to work with your companions and allow no gaps to form in the line. It is permissible to lift the pace gradually and if this results in people being dropped then they have been ridden off your wheel and are of no use to the bunch anyway. If you are behind someone who jumps on the pedals when they hit the front do not reprimand the offender with cries of 'Don't Surge' unless the offender is a Frenchman named Serge.

I think we all know someone called Serge. Or Sergio. There are several of these guys in just about every bunch ever formed. But don't hold them to judgement, gently take them aside and explain the intricacies, the subtleties and the simple mechanics of rotating the group and keeping everyone at the same comfortable pace. When the penny drops, and they integrate with the smooth workings of their co-conspirators, it's a beautiful sight to behold and an even more beautiful one to be part of.

Here's a simple rundown. You're riding two abreast on the front of the group, and you're the outside rider (closest to the traffic). You find yourself listening to some prat going on about heart rates or metres climbed. You have to get out of there. At this stage, you should verbally announce you are 'rolling over', which means pulling ahead of the rider next to you with a slight increase in pace, then pulling across to the front position immediately in front of the rider who was beside. That rider should have kept the pace the same as it was before the other rider rolled over. The following riders on the traffic side all move up one position. The rider on the outside in the back does the reverse and moves into the last position in the other line.

Sound complicated? Remember that practice makes perfect, that common sense is essential and that it's easier to do than it is to explain. Cyclists are crap writers, after all.

RULE #92 //
NO SPRINTING FROM THE HOODS

The only exception is riders whose name starts with Guiseppe and ends with Saronni. If you can win the World Championship Rainbow Stripes sprinting from the hoods, you have earned yourself a lifetime absolution.

Yes, his brake levers were almost on the drops of his bars already and yes, he was sprinting uphill. Many have tried but few have succeeded attempting this.

"Beppe" Saronni was another in the legion of dark-haired, dark-eyed, handsome Italian racers, except he became a World Champion. His win in 1982 at Goodwood, England, was controversial only for the crushed riders he left behind him. While the Americans were busy going too early and chasing each other down, Saronni unleashed a long uphill sprint from the brake hoods that left no doubt who deserved to wear the Rainbow Jersey.

Every cyclist must have a sprint, no exceptions. If you and a mate are heading for a town line, you'd better be ready to drop the hammer the moment you hear a gear-shift. Your sprint might be wobbly and weak but you never know, your mate's may be wobblier and weaker. It is completely unacceptable to simply sit up and say, *Go on then, I don't have a sprint*. You'd better find a sprint and find a proper one, that starts and ends with your hands on the drops of your handlebars. Your hands and arms are at the ready to counter the massive power each leg is administering to the rear wheel. Holding on to the tops of the bars or the brake hoods is not going to work, unless your objective lies somewhere in the gutter.

When your hands go to the drops, your ass comes up out of the saddle, with every bit of power and weight available going to the cranks. Grab those bars low, elbows bent, jacking the bars side to side, the body pulled down and forward. A sprinter once told me the secret to a good sprint is trying to break the handlebars.

This Rule is more important now than ever. With Group-san brake levers sticking up above the tops of the bars like ski pole grips, even Jens Voigt gets a locker-room towel-snapping for trying such an amateur stunt.

This Rule was suggested by a man who knows a thing or two about getting outsprinted by Beppe Saronni, Scotland's Robert Millar. Millar, an extremely classy rider in his own right, would have shown Saronni some rear wheel on any steep Dolomite or Pyrenean climb, but never in a sprint and never from the hoods.

No-one makes it into the professional ranks without winning some important sprints and you can bet that any uphill sprints Robert Millar contested, his hands were firmly on the drops of his bars.

PART III:
The Bike

'A good bicycle and its components are beautiful things to me. I'm not just talking about appearance, but also how the frame and components show the dreams of those who made them.'

Gianni Bugno, Italian Hardman
and Cycling legend

The bicycle is the central tool of our craft. This beautiful machine loyally serves as our vehicle to La Vie Velominatus, offering suffering and pleasure in equal measure, and must be respected for giving us this gift. Its basic elements epitomise the beauty of simplicity, yet can be curated to meet our personal specifications, demands or whims.

As we progress along the path of La Vie Velominatus, we find ourselves increasingly obsessed with individual components and the merits of their selection. It begins, perhaps, with new bar tape or a change of saddle. The component itself isn't important; what is important is that our own two hands installed it and the choice to do so came from within. After making a change, perhaps the machine caught our eye in a way it hadn't before; there was something about it that had until then been hidden. A new world opens before us that can hardly be comprehended before this first step is taken.

Bicycles, first and foremost, are to be ridden. Whether on sunny boulevards or in torrential rain; the only thing worse than a dirty, poorly cared-for bike is an immaculate bike that goes unused. But once it finds its way onto the road routinely, the bicycle is to be meticulously loved and cared for. If it becomes dirty, it shall be promptly cleaned. If something breaks, it must be mended. If the bar tape or saddle wears, it will be replaced.

Maintaining a bicycle is an art, and also a means of transcendence. It is a simple machine, one whose moving bits and components can be examined and understood. Most any part can be removed or installed with a simple hex key or wrench; all that is required to clean it is a rag, some soapy water and a drop of oil for the chain. Adjusting brakes and derailleurs involves nothing more than a gentle turn of a barrel adjuster to find the right tension. Yet to do so perfectly takes time and practice; a good bicycle mechanic is an artisan, not a labourer or engineer.

Similarly, a classic bicycle wheel can be built with basic tools; spokes are inserted into the hub following a simple pattern, and through an extension of the pattern they are connected to the rim. The wheel takes shape as spokes are tensioned and before long the wheel emerges from what was a disparate collection of hub, spokes and rim. Yet to build a wheel that stays true and round requires patience and skill; a perfectly built wheel should never lose its shape and those who are most closely able to reach this perfection are those who build the most durable wheels. This is a skill that commands a premium and it is in short supply.

There are few joys in life that surpass working on a bicycle. The bike and rider bond through this process and learn to know each other on a level entirely different from scaling a high mountain pass or a hallowed cobbled track. Through caring for the machine, we learn to love it anew, to memorise the sound each component makes when finely tuned and when it requires adjustment or replacement. There is an inverse relationship between the frequency with which a bicycle part needs our attention and the emotional connection we feel toward said part. Tubes are at one end of the spectrum. We inspect and inflate our tyres' pressure prior to each ride and replace tubes on a regular basis. And while we can appreciate and extol the virtues of butyl versus latex or various patches, our attachment to the tube never really goes beyond utilitarian. For the tubular rider, the connection to the tyre perhaps goes a level deeper due to the superior ride quality and higher care needed to replace a tyre, especially if the wheel is adorned with something like an FMB Paris–Roubaix. But in the final analysis, this connection is still not as deep as with components further up the spectrum. Moving further along, we have longer lasting bits such as chains, cassettes, cables and bar tape. All of these bely the commitment of the Velominatus to his or her machine through the quality chosen and attention to their curation on the bike. Bar tape alone can speak volumes about how dedicated one is to riding the path of the Velominati. Moving still further, we have more permanent fixtures such as the contact points between rider and machine. The selection of the saddle, pedals, shoes and handlebars is where the lines between style, fit and function begin to blur even further. And lastly, the most important choices are those concerning the *gruppo*, wheels and frame-set. These are the components that say something about the rider; their dedication to the sport, the craft and the art of Cycling. The *gruppo*, wheels and frame are not only how the rider will identify their bike but also how they will identify *with* their bike.

The bicycle, above all else, is something to be loved.

RULE #8 //
SADDLES, BARS, AND TYRES
SHALL BE CAREFULLY
MATCHED

Valid options are:

- Match the saddle to the bars and the tyres to black; or
- Match the bars to the colour of the frame at the top of the head tube and the saddle to the colour of the frame at the top of the seat tube and the tyres to the colour where they come closest to the frame; or
- Match the saddle and the bars to the frame decals; or
- Black, black, black

What makes you believe it's acceptable to ride your red bike shod with yellow bar tape, a blue saddle and mismatched tyres? A technicolour dreamcoat your bike is not. You are a Cycling ambassador, and in that capacity it is your primary responsibility to Look Fantastic at All Times. Your bike is an extension of you and your personality, and as such should be immaculately presented. Just as you brush your teeth and comb your hair (if you have any), grooming your bike should be as natural a task as those basic actions.

Black, black, black. As in fashion, it's a go-to solution to any dressing problem we may encounter. Shirt, trousers, shoes and socks all look good if they're the same colour.

And black is the easiest colour there is to work with. The same principle applies to your bike; if you're not quite sure whether the white tape/red saddle combo will work, it won't. On the other hand, your bike will look smart no matter what its frame colour may be, as long as the tape, saddle and tyres are kept basic black.

White is relatively easy to work with too, even if it doesn't possess the set-and-forget simplicity of its opposite hue. Keeping white bar tape clean can be a chore, but a necessary one if you choose to run it. Once again, look to your sartorial guidelines; you wouldn't wear a white shirt replete with brown underarm stains, so there's no excuse to justify riding around with dirty, once-white bar tape. It's one of the most common faux pas among recreational Cyclists and the most easily preventable. If you lack the discipline to keep your bar tape white, then it's time to go black.

As for other colours, while generally frowned upon they can be made to work in some circumstances. Take Pantani's 98 Giro/Tour double-winning Bianchi as a prime example of impeccable colour-matching. While celeste and yellow would no doubt present a neon nightmare for most of us, the way in which Il Pirata presented his machine was the work of a master. This is to be used as an extreme example only and should not be attempted at home unless you happen to have one of those beautiful machines in your possession. And if you do, you'd better be able to climb in the big ring with your hands in the drops to honour the master of Rule #8.

RULE #26 //
MAKE YOUR BIKE PHOTOGENIC

When photographing your bike, gussy her up properly for the camera. Some parameters are firm: valve stems at 6 o'clock. Cranks never at 90 or 180 degrees. Other details are at your discretion, though the accepted practices include putting the chain on the big dog and no bidons in the cages.

Bicycles, as we've established, are objects of beauty. We love not only to ride them, but to touch them, smell them, hear them hum, and of course to look at them.

There exists no more elegant tool for sporting pursuits than the bicycle. Its simple, clean lines have been around since the invention of the 'safety bicycle' in the 1880's. The double diamond frame is simplicity personified, especially when forged from the original material of choice, round steel tubes, either joined by mitring and welding or by the most beautiful form of bringing tubes together, the lug. Lugs can be formed into intricate entities, complete with scalloping and flowing lines into which the tubes fit, and are then brazed by the delicate, heated touch of the artisan frame-builder.

Modern-day bicycles have morphed into more varied shapes and carbon fibre frames can be formed into any non-conventional shape imaginable. Some are just as beautiful

= unused

as their metal predecessors, while others have fallen out the ugly tree and hit every branch on the way down. But no matter what material a bicycle is made from, or what shapes the tubes are, or what colour it is painted, we can all agree that beauty is indeed in the eye of the beholder. Like a red-headed stepchild, every bike will eventually find love in one form or another.

When it comes to photographing your loved ones, be they your child, grandparents or even pets, you'll usually take care to ensure that everyone is looking at the camera, their hair neat, and smiling the widest of grins. Maybe you'll tell a joke in order to put everyone at ease, or demand that they all say 'Cheese'. Regardless of your method, you require the composition to be just right. The same applies to your bike. Don't just throw it against a wall and snap away. Pick a background that is not too busy and distracting from the subject. Photograph the bike from the drive side. Shift the chain to the big ring and a small cog. Get those valve stems at 6 o'clock. The non-drive crank should be level with the chainstay or seat tube – or bisect the two perfectly. Telling it a joke probably won't have any effect, but it will make those witnessing an adult talking to a bicycle chuckle.

Now steady your camera and say 'Campyyyyy.'

RULE #29 //
NO EUROPEAN POSTERIOR MAN-SATCHELS

Saddlebags have no place on a road bike, and are only acceptable on mountain bikes in extreme cases.

Similar to many of the great debates throughout history – the chicken or the egg, toilet paper rolled from the front or back, Tour vs Giro – Rule #29 has garnered fervoured zealots on either side of the issue. But make no mistake, saddlebags were put onto this earth by The Prophet for one reason only: to test your faith.

Perhaps no other Rule has been violated so flagrantly and debated so vigorously as this. After all, it is tempting to besmirch your steed with a saddlebag as you feel the weight and bulge of jersey pockets increasing. Resist. Resist as a matter of aesthetics and out of respect for your bike. No matter how slim, 'integrated' or practical you think that European Posterior Man-Satchel is, it will spoil the lines of your bike and gnaw at your conscience as you strive for compliance.

The fundamental principle at the core of the argument is: what are you carrying all that gear for? Road Cycling is about simplicity, not portaging a team's worth of supplies with you. A well-maintained bicycle requires very little equipment for a ride: a tube or two, a mini-pump; a set of tyre levers and a mini-tool. On a long ride, you would be forgiven a few morsels of food, but that collection of gear will hardly bring your pockets to the point of bursting. If you are riding with a minimized set of tools and still find your pockets to be sagging, consider changing the size of your jersey; your kit should fit properly, and properly fitting kit doesn't sag, even with tools and food stowed in your pockets.

Whatever your excuse is, it has been heard and thoroughly debunked before. Here are a few examples:

'I already have too much in my jersey pockets with my patch kit, multi-tool, food, mobile phone, and mini-pump.' No, that's exactly what you should have in your jersey pockets and why you have three of them.

'My ride takes me far from home and if I have a mechanical I'm screwed so I need more tools.' Maintain your bike. If you need a headset press midway through an eight-hour suffer-fest, have someone maintain your bike who knows what they're doing because you clearly don't.

'I'm not a pro and therefore I'm not followed by a team car.' Are you trying to fit a spare wheelset and a *directeur sportif* in your EPMS?

'I live in a place where it is very [hot/cold] and therefore I need to carry more [water/food/clothes]'. Everyone lives somewhere that makes us prone to be a whiny little bitch. Drop what you're doing and meditate on Rule #5. Do not pass Go, do not collect £200.

RULE #30 //
NO FRAME-MOUNTED
PUMPS

Either CO_2 canisters or mini-pumps should be carried in jersey pockets (See Rule #31). The only exception to this Rule is to mount a Silca-brand frame pump in the rear triangle of the frame, with the rear wheel-skewer as the pump mount nob, as demonstrated by members of the 7-Eleven and Ariostea Pro Cycling teams. As such, a frame pump mounted upside down and along the left (skewer-lever side) seat stay is both old-school and Euro and thus acceptable. We restate at this time that said pump may under no circumstances be a Zefal and must be made by Silca. Said Silca pump must be fitted with a Campagnolo head. It is acceptable to gaffer-tape a mini-pump to your frame when no CO_2 canisters are available and your pockets are full of spare kit and energy gels. However, the rider should expect to be stopped and questioned and may be required to empty pockets to prove there is no room in them for the pump.

With recent advances in technology, the shape of the tubes atop which we sit and pedal have evolved into curved, bent and ovalised forms, far from what the traditional outline of a bicycle was in years gone by. And while the old way to inflate a tyre was by a long, thin handpump, today we are blessed with tiny air-movers small enough to fit comfortably in our jersey pocket and still get a tube filled to 100psi in the time it used to take to unclip the frame-mounted pump from your bike. What's more, we don't even have to pump at all if we don't want to, we can just screw on a CO_2-filled cartridge and blow that sucker up in a matter of seconds. Wow!

Sometimes these newfangled instant inflators can let us down though, and a botched threading of a cartridge can result in the gas being lost to the atmosphere for ever, its only contribution being to the ever-increasing hole in the ozone layer. Which means you should still carry a pump. And while we're not going to deny that a big old Silca that nestles between the head and seat tubes will get you up to pressure a fair bit quicker than something resembling a baby carrot with a hose attached, we also observe that you can't fit that thing in your flash modern frame.

Even those little pumps that resemble a chromed gherkin can be 'frame-mounted' but this is even more troublesome to the aesthete's eye. The bracket used to affix the pump next to the bidon cage should be put to re-use as landfill or on your workshop pegboard to hold a screwdriver or CO_2 canister. It has no place on your bicycle.

Of course, you could always ride with someone so set in their old-skool ways that should you suffer the dreaded hissss, you can just borrow their big frame pump. Be sure to tell them how awesome it is though, and that if you had a 25-year-old bike you'd definitely be getting one of those cool pumps too.

RULE #34 //
MOUNTAIN BIKE
SHOES AND PEDALS HAVE
THEIR PLACE

On a mountain bike.

Shimano Pedaling Dynamics (SPD) pedals for road bikes were introduced in the early 1990s, a road shoe with an inset cleat. A road shoe that made walking normal and practical. The Japanese, surprisingly, must have a low tolerance for embarrassment to even think of such a design. Normality and practicality are overrated.

Most mountain bike shoes are road shoes with a burlier sole. Mountain bike pedals are engineered to work in muddy, filthy conditions. By design they are a little loose and sloppy, what the manufacturers might market as 'float'. They are an imperfect interface between bike and human. Like a poor electrical connection, signal is lost. An imperfect human/ bicycle unit is unacceptable.

There is no shame in pushing a mountain bike or cyclocross bike up a muddy grade: that is what mountain bike shoes are designed for – pushing your bike. If you need to push your bike, it better not be a road bike.

A road Cyclist will never push their ride up any incline. No matter how steep the grade and how overgeared your bike, you must ride up it. If baby noises and wretched curse words tumble from your mouth, muffled by the chunks of bar tape in your teeth, it's still better than walking. The inconvenience of staying off the bike for two weeks with a bung knee is nothing compared to the lifelong stain of having taken the Walk of Shame.

If you really can't make it up because you are a big pussy and have not yet fully embraced The V, do this: make like Tommy Simpson, minus the dying part. You and bike keel over together and you implore whoever is in earshot to 'Put me back on my bike, put me back on my bike!' With any luck they will, and give you a decent push to get you moving towards the top again.

RULE #40 //
TYRES ARE TO BE MOUNTED WITH THE LABEL CENTERED OVER THE VALVE STEM

Pro mechanics do this because it makes it easier to find the valve. You do this because that's the way pro mechanics do it. This will save you precious seconds while your fat ass sits on the roadside fumbling with your CO_2 after a flat. It also looks better for photo opportunities. Note: This obviously only applies to clinchers as tubulars don't give you a choice.

If you are hip enough to be riding sew-ups, please move along. But before you move on, I have a question. Are you really patching your own tubular tyres? You are? OK, now you can go. Everyone else in the world, the clincher and tubeless-tyre users, please listen up. Purely on aesthetic grounds, Rule #40 is a good and fair Rule. In a disorderly world, order is good.

This is not some OCD whimsy floated down from Mt Velomis. The aligned tyre label and valve stem idea has been around for many years; we don't make these things up. Wheels look better when the tyre label and valve stem are aligned. We choose to put the tyre graphics right over the valve stem hole. Once the inner tube is installed and inflated, the final product is a very squared away looking wheel. Put two wheels like that on your bike and it's halfway to Looking Fantastic.

There is also a rationale behind this, if you are too afraid to do it for the look alone. When you get a puncture, knowing where your inner tube and tyre were in relation to each other is very useful in hunting down either the hole in the tube or the offending puncturing item still hiding in the tyre. The label also makes it easy to find the valve stem for inflating, and may provide valuable pressure statistics should you require them.

Scanning a line-up of bikes against a wall, a bike in Rule #40 compliance stands proud and declares 'My owner is inside getting pissed with his friends. His life may well be a series of bad career moves and even worse relationship moves. He never sends in his tax forms on time and he never calls his mother. However, he does love me and lives La Vie Velominatus.'

RULE #41 //
QUICK-RELEASE
LEVERS ARE TO BE
CAREFULLY POSITIONED

Quick-release angle on the front skewer shall be an upward angle that tightens just aft of the fork and the rear quick release shall tighten at an angle that bisects the angle between the seat and chainstays. It is acceptable, however, to have the rear quick release tighten upward, just aft of the seat stay, when the construction of the frame or its dropouts will not allow the preferred positioning. For time-trial bikes only, quick releases may be in the horizontal position facing towards the rear of the bike. This is for maximum aero effect.

The Campagnolo quick-release, positioned perfectly, is perhaps the most iconic bit of kit.

La Vie Velominatus expresses itself through the details. Just as tyres should be mounted with the labels positioned carefully over the valve stems, the positioning of quick-release levers is a signal that the owner of the machine is well versed in doing things properly.

As before, if you absolutely must have a reason beyond 'shut up and do it', then I submit the following; these positions minimise the risk of having a foreign object dislodge the skewer and cause your wheel to depart the frame at a possibly inconvenient and certainly surprising moment. These positions also allow the frame or fork to act as a leverage point for your wimpy hand as you squeeze the lever shut and later pry it open.

RULE #48 //
SADDLES MUST BE LEVEL
AND PUSHED BACK

The seating area of a saddle is to be visually level, with the base measurement made using a spirit level. Based on subtleties of saddle design and requirements of comfort, the saddle may then be pitched slightly forward or backward to reach a position that offers stability, power and comfort. If the tilt of the saddle exceeds two degrees, you need to go get one of those saddles with springs and a thick gel pad because you are obviously a big pussy.

The midpoint of the saddle as measured from tip to tail shall fall well behind and may not be positioned forward of the line made by extending the seat tube through the top of the saddle. (Also see Rule #44.)

Our Lord Merckx seemed always to be fiddling with his seat height, whipping out a tape measure and an Allen wrench at the slightest provocation. Apparently there are no translations in French nor Flemish for 'set and forget'. But he was never screwing with the angle of his saddle – a truly sensitive adjustment, arguably more so than saddle height.

A slight change of seat angle has a direct effect on how the rider's weight is distributed between saddle and handlebars. Tilt the nose of the saddle down a bit and suddenly much more weight goes on the bars. The bike's handling changes; it corners differently, less easily, less smoothly. The rider's arms will be supporting too much torso weight; it's all off, a mess. Tilting the saddle nose up a hair can take a little weight off the front end. All these minor adjustments depend on the rider's build, but the correct place to start is with a level saddle. A spirit level helps to reproduce an adjustment and accurately measure minor tweaks.

Cycling mythology has passed down many nuggets of sage yet questionable wisdom, none with less scientific foundation than fore and aft seat position. Over the millennia, hunting for proper seat position has involved the use of plumb-bobs, knee caps, crank angles and pedal axles.

Steve Bauer, who in 1984 became the first Canadian to win an Olympic medal in road Cycling, had the Merckx factory build him a radical frame for the 1993 Paris–Roubaix race. Steve wanted to test a notion he had about an extreme rearward seat position engaging the quadriceps more efficiently, thus producing more power to the pedals.

Let's just say Steve didn't finish in the top ten that year and the bike never reappeared.

There is no definitive formula to derive the optimum fore and aft seat position. Femur-to-tibia ratios might be a place to start but there is no place to finish. A fitting system like Retül relies on a database of Cyclists' body/bike measurements rather than an exact position calculator. They are looking at the majority of Cyclists who have ridden before us over the years to arrive at an optimum position.

In summary: the centre of the saddle should be set behind the centre of the seat pin and be level front to back. All adjustments from this starting position should be to maximise both comfort and power. It all is merely a refinement of position toward the V-Locus.

RULE #54 //
NO AEROBARS
ON ROAD BIKES

Aerobars or other clip-on attachments are under no circumstances to be employed on your road bike. The only exception to this is if you are competing in a mountain time trial.

It all started with Greg LeMond. No, not the specialisation on a particular race, as he was a renowned all-season racer. Nor being an American wading into a big, Euro-dominated pond that was the pro circuit in the 80s. What he was a true pioneer of was the aero revolution.

When he rolled out of the start-house for his historic time trial in the 1989 Tour, few gave him much chance of over-hauling the 50-second deficit to his great rival, the Frenchman Laurent Fignon. Even fewer counted on him showing up with a set of handlebars unlike any seen before in the European peloton. But by the end of the 24.5-km final stage, plenty were taking a lot more notice. What came after would rival the arms race happening around the same time between the USA and Russia. Weapons of race construction were being churned out at a rate of speed that would match LeMan's velocity on the Champs Elysées that fateful, famous day.

What he had mounted to his more traditional bullhorn bars looked like something that you might spot on a walking frame, such was their crudeness. The idea was simple: get into a tuck position much like a downhill skier to minimise frontal area as much as possible, thus reducing wind resistance. Whether the bars were the deciding factor in the race, or Greg's amazing capacity to ride at the limits of his power output, or Fignon's pony tail and double disc wheels, we'll never really know. What we do know is he started a trend that continues in time-trialling to the present day. He also birthed an abomination that has seen its way onto the front ends of all types of bikes that should never be seen with such pipework adorning them.

For a while, aerobars were allowed in one-day races and road-race stages of Grand Tours. But this presented a new problem; when a rider's grip on the bars is narrowed into an aero position, their hands are far away from the brakes, the steering of the bike is compromised and controlling the machine in a situation where there are up to 200 people riding butt to nose to shoulder, it becomes much more of an issue than if you are barrelling into a corner at speed, all alone and can pick whatever line you please. While the type of aerobars were more compact than those typically used in a time trial (i.e. Spinaci bars), there was an increase in sketchiness within the peloton that couldn't be ignored. Mostly on the grounds of safety, they were banned from mass-start events.

Triathletes, always looking for a way to suck less than they always will, adopted the bars en masse and took them to even more ridiculous levels of bardom. This was just about acceptable for the longer distance races where drafting was forbidden and some advantage could be taken, but in shorter races where pack riding was permissible, their already suspect handling skills (most were predominantly runners and swimmers, after all) were compromised even further. When tri-geeks started turning up for bunch rides and tucking themselves into their ridiculous aero positions, roadies would smartly scold them for their stupidity or banish them from the ride altogether.

So then we had a situation of lone tri-geeks and wannabe time-trialists riding through traffic in their aero tucks, latching on to groups or trying to hammer past while having their heads down and asses up. Commuters saw this and thought they could make their 3km trip to work that bit faster and started bolting pipework onto their mountain bikes and hybrids. In addition to not giving them any benefit at all due to their pannier-laden bikes and wide bellies, they looked ever more stupid as their Yellow Jackets of Authority flapped in the wind, backpacks creating a hump that would give a camel a boner, and knobby tyres buzzing along the tarmac like a chainsaw on a sheet-metal floor.

There is no valid reason to mount aerobars on a road bike, unless you use it to race Time Trials. Besides the fact that you're too slow for it to matter, the beautiful, simple lines of the bike should in no way be sullied with these hideous contraptions. Get in the drops, flatten your back De Vlaeminck-style and not only will you gain a greater aero advantage, you won't run the risk of looking like a skier who's lost his poles.

RULE #57 //
NO STICKERS

Nobody gives a shit what causes you support, what war you're against, what gear you buy or what year you rode L'Etape du Tour. See Rule #5 and ride your bike. Decals, on the other hand, are not only permissible, but also extremely pro.

Stickers are for toolboxes, not bicycles. Respect your machine: keep it clean, well-maintained and sticker-free. Decals, however, can be badass and a worthy addition to your machine. A strategically placed V-cal on the top tube says to the world, 'We ain't here to piss around, this bike and me, we're here to ride. Let's boogie.'

RULE #60 //
DITCH THE WASHER-NUT AND VALVE-STEM CAP

You are not, under any circumstances, to employ the use of the washer-nut and valve-stem cap that come with your inner tubes or tubulars. They are only supplied to meet shipping regulations. They are useless when it comes to tubes and tyres.

You'd be surprised how many people go into bike shops and ask if they can have some valve caps because they've lost theirs. They exhibit an irrational fear that air will be making a beeline for the atmosphere if the little black plastic teat isn't safely screwed on. Rather than start lecturing the uninformed as to the uselessness of the caps, or preaching some obscure Rule to them, the bike-shop guys will have a ready-made stash for such occasions. They realise these people can't be helped, so they are set free with a half dozen caps, eternally thankful and amazed that they didn't even have to pay for them.

You though, you know better. Or if you don't, you should. In either case, it goes no further; it stops here. The Presta valve is a wonderful piece of engineering, designed to hold air by means of a screw-down cap that closes the valve. But dirt might get in there, I hear you say. No, not unless it can unthread a nut somehow. Maybe radioactive dirt in Russia, but that's rare and while radioactive dirt might also give you More Massive Guns, we'll take our chances.

As for the valve-stem washer-nut, well, it can serve a purpose if you have mistakenly bought a tube with a too-short valve and you need it to hold the valve while you get some semblance of pump head to suckle it. Then you chuck it, or save it for the next lost hipster that wanders your way.

There is a bike shop in Seattle called Speedy Reedy that has a giant bell hanging over the workbench with an enormous pail underneath it; every time an inner tube loses its nut, it goes into the pail and the bell is rung. You might think about installing a smaller one on your own workbench.

RULE #61 //
LIKE YOUR GUNS, SADDLES SHOULD BE SMOOTH AND HARD

Under no circumstances may your saddle have more than 3mm of padding. Special allowances will be made for stage racing when physical pain caused by subcutaneous cysts and the like ('saddle sores') are present. Under those conditions, up to 5mm of padding will be allowed. It should be noted that this exception is only temporary until the condition has passed or been excised. A hardman would not change their saddle at all but instead cut a hole in it to relieve pressure on the delicate area. It is noted that if Rule #48 and/or Rule #5 is observed then any 'padding' is superfluous.

You're halfway through a long, hot day, your legs and lungs are burning from the heat and the generous helpings of Rule #5 you've clinically administered to them. You're dangling off the back on all the climbs, and you've run out of food already in your hurried attempts to stave off the Man with the Hammer. But none of this is really registering on the V-Meter, as there is a searing, friction-fuelled pain screaming at you from a place you don't want to be thinking about in the big scheme of things. You have been training for this ride with the fervour of a rabid dog, and now the hours of saddle time and some unwashed bibs have come back to bite you on the ass. Literally.

As Cyclists, we are prone to developing a painful cyst in the seating area that is lovingly referred to as a 'saddle sore'. While uncomfortable, the development of a saddle sore is a rite of passage, a badge we wear that tells instantly of our devotion to The Work. While we don't go around showing it off, the mere mention of one elicits nods of understanding from fellow Velominati.

Legends are told of this ugly side of our sport that will shrink your testicles (if you have them) to the size of raisins. Laurent Fignon had a painful sore for which he hacked a hole in his saddle in order to limit the friction caused by the pistoning of his Massive Guns. Sean Kelly, it is said, once asked his *soigneur* to lance a boil that had developed during the Vuelta a España. Kelly, perhaps the most stoic man to ever throw a leg over a top tube, is said to have shrieked like a teenage girl in a slasher flick during the operation, which was ultimately aborted. It was so painful that he withdrew from the race two days before the finish, while leading.

No amount of mental toughness can overcome this most heinous of Cycling 'injuries'. You might recall Oscar Freire cutting a chunk out of his perch to accommodate the golf ball lodged in his taint in the Tour those years ago. You conjure images of Tom Boonen stuffing extra padding down his bibs to create a makeshift diaper and ease the pressure on his third, pus-filled testicle, also at la Vuelta. And you quickly dismiss both notions, neither wanting to destroy your new Arione nor to draw even more scorn than usual when you ponce your way into the café at the end of the ride. You consider one of those seats with a cut-out, and maybe taking some time off the bike.

Are you fucking insane? Time off the bike? Granted,

sometimes rest is the best medicine for over-V'ed Cyclists, some time to replenish The V-Bank and freshen up the guns so you can come out swinging again. But letting a little crotch pimple ruin your fun? Not happening. Think of Robbie McEwen talking about how to squeeze that sucker and douse its Anti-V-bodies with some neat whisky – or maybe it was rubbing alcohol, but whisky sounds better. OK, it's going to send you through the roof in teeth-clenching, deity-cursing agony but if Robbie did it, you know it's gonna work. Take a couple of deep breaths, then drink the rest of the whisky. Pain? What pain? Let's go dancing.

When you've returned to sobriety and can think clearly once more, take a second to reflect on that other 'solution' you considered. If you are going to entertain the thought of mounting a cut-out saddle on your bike, then pick up some handlebar streamers and a wicker basket while you're at the LBS, because they'll help just as much at making your ride any better as one of those peek-a-boo-hoo seats will. If anything, the extra edges created by a cut-out will contribute to more friction and increased pressure, thus more chance of cultivating an ingrown-hair pus-ball.

There is no magic saddle out there; everyone has different nether regions and what works for some won't for others. Trial and error is the only way. You'll know long before any bacteria have a chance to do their thing downstairs if a saddle is right for you. Get a suitable width and shape; padding bears a lot less importance. Good quality bibshorts are key, but keeping them fresh is even more so; wash them after every ride and repeat. Also, take a note out of the porn star handbook, because no one gets more mileage downtown than they do; hair just adds friction, so keep the hedges trimmed.

The best advice for the happiness of this delicate area is to ride lots and build up armour down below. Nothing beats having a ride-toughened taint that can repel saddle sores by reputation alone.

RULE #65 //
MAINTAIN AND RESPECT
YOUR MACHINE

Your Bicycle must adhere to the *Principle of Silence* and as such must be meticulously maintained. It must be cherished, and when leaning it against a wall, must be leaned carefully such that only the bars, saddle or tyres come in contact with the wall or post. This is true even when dismounting prior to collapsing after the World Championship Time Trial. No squeaks, creaks or chain noise allowed. Only the soothing hum of your tyres upon the tarmac and the rhythm of your breathing may be audible when riding. When riding the Pavé, the sound of chain slap is acceptable. The Principle of Silence can be extended to say that if you are suffering such that your breathing begins to adversely effect the enjoyment of the other riders in the bunch, you are to summarily sit up and allow yourself to be dropped.

Who could let this Royce hub and Campag cassette stay dirty for long?

The condition of your bicycle is much more than a direct reflection of the regard in which you hold it. It is a reflection of your dedication to La Vie Velominatus, to how you approach the craft of Cycling and ultimately how you live your life off the bike. This most sacred of tools demands your undying dedication. Some say that the bicycle is merely a means to an end, a tool to be expended and replaced. These are the same people whose drivetrains sound like military track vehicles stuck in the mud of Flanders' fields and whose handlebar tape looks like a dog's tattered toy.

They may ride well but they would ride better if they properly maintained their bikes. Just as a chef sharpens his knives, a painter teases frayed hairs from her brush and a mason cleans the excess mortar from a screed, the Cycling Disciple must remain steadfastly meticulous in caring for their bicycles.

The Prophet himself painstakingly looked after his own stable. It is said that his livery had over thirty-five bicycles, fifteen of which were in impeccable condition and ready to ride at any given time. Countless other riders as well have demonstrated their dedication to their machines. Greg LeMond famously spirited away one of his early carbon bikes to his hotel room to look after it during the 1991 Tour. This led his mechanics to believe for some time that it was stolen. There are other tales of Cyclists aging tyres in their wine cellars, using only extra virgin Italian olive oil as chain lubricant and calling on other riders in the peloton to silence their noisy, unkempt machines.

Every squeak, creak and click is not only a sign of your bike needing care, it is a harbinger of inefficiency and wasted energy. Those micro-watts it takes to turn that creaking crank spindle ten thousand times over a long day add up. Not to mention the mental toll it takes on you and your mates as you suffer through the noise. There are countless forces that conspire to sap a potentially great ride. Many of those forces can be controlled or at least influenced by the riders, while some cannot. Maintaining your bike is one force that you can exert virtually total control over.

For the Velominatus just beginning to walk the path, any maintenance task beyond the fixing of a flat or lubing of a chain may seem as daunting as climbing l'Alpe d'Huez in the 53x11. But just as you muster all your *grinta* to begin turning the pedals on a Rule #9 day, you must begin to learn to properly care for your machine. Over time you will gain an intimate knowledge of each cog, bearing, race, bolt and cable. Tracking down noises and diagnosing problems will become second nature. For the Disciple to truly develop into a Velominata, she must not only learn but also take joy in the care and upkeep of her bike.

If none of this is convincing enough, take a good look at any piece of a Campagnolo *gruppo* and then ask yourself if Tulli Campagnolo ever intended it to stay dirty for very long. As with any piece of functional art, it works best and induces the most appreciation when cared for by capable, respectful and loving hands.

**Don't be averse to your bike getting dirty.
Just clean it afterwards.**

RULE #66 //
NO MIRRORS

Mirrors are allowed on your (aptly named) Surly Big Dummy or your Surly Long Haul Trucker. Not on your road steed. Not on your mountain bike. Not on your helmet. If someone familiar with The Rules has sold you such an abomination, return the mirror and demand a refund, plus interest and damages.

What is it, precisely, that you're trying to spy back there? And what, precisely, is it you plan to do when you spot it?

The mirror is a vestige from the automobile; a bicycle is a different thing entirely. You can actually see around it quite well simply by moving your head.

The Cyclist must learn to absorb their surroundings through using their senses – peripheral vision, sound and smell. Like a Jedi uses the Force, we become one with the environment we find ourselves in – the road, the traffic furniture, pedestrians and animals at the roadside – and learn to anticipate what is going to happen around us.

Indeed, we must become one with our machine and navigate through obstacles as if the machine was a part of our very being.

Most importantly, mirrors are ugly.

RULE #69 //
CYCLING SHOES AND BICYCLES ARE MADE FOR RIDING

Any walking conducted while wearing Cycling shoes must be strictly limited. When taking a slash or filling bidons during a 200km ride (at 38kmh: see Rule #68) one is to carefully stow one's bicycle at the nearest point navigable by bike and walk the remaining distance. It is strictly prohibited under any circumstances that a Cyclist should walk up a steep incline, with the obvious exception being when said incline is blocked by riders who crashed because you are on the Koppenberg. For clarification, see Rule #5.

Cycling shoes are in no way made for walking. They only work when spinning pedals. A Cyclist loathes walking in all its forms. And to make sure we are terrible at it, we always have metal and hard plastic attached to the soles of our shoes, our anti-walking skids. Walking is slow enough as it is, but walking in Cycling shoes is hazardous to our health. If there were more ride-through liquor stores (one of America's proudest inventions) we'd never even have to go to the shops.

Time pedals have long been an icon of the sport, known for an all-metal cleat that was suicidal in cafés. Many a charming rouleur strode into a local watering hole, ready to impress the pretty lady in the corner by being such a virile athlete, only to wipe out and take down a few curtains after hitting a half-damp patch of floor. *Time* remedied this by inventing the 'Cafe Cleat', incorporating rubber on the outside of the cleat so you couldn't blame them for not getting the girl. It's a proud moment in every road Cyclist's life when they first skitter and fall to the ground on the varnished hardwood floor of a shop. 'No, I'm not pissed; I'm a Cyclist.'

Yes, you are a Cyclist; you are different because you are made to ride, not walk. You are incomplete without your bike. In a café, clutching at ale bottles, you fall where no one else ever would. What's the alternative, to violate Rule #34? Do you think doing that would enable you to stride into a store without careful mincing steps? That's one step closer to being normal. It's standing on the outskirts of our tribal village, almost in the dark jungle, lost, away from our people.

RULE #73 //
GEAR AND BRAKE CABLES SHOULD BE CUT TO OPTIMUM LENGTH

Cables should create a perfect arc around the head tube and, whenever possible, cross under the down tube. Right shifter cable should go to the left cable stop and vice versa.

We'll start Rule #73 by sharing the story of a friend. A great guy, a more than solid rider, earns a nice pay packet, loves riding his bikes. But to look at him, you'd be forgiven for thinking he was either blind, destitute or creating some sort of avant-garde instalment with his steed as the centrepiece. Bits of duct tape, Velcro, clear protective strips and what look suspiciously like tube repair patches stuck all over the frame to keep the cables from rubbing the paintwork. The effort of keeping his bikes looking like new made them look instead like a double-diamond turd that someone had thrown up on. Maybe that's a bit harsh, but they looked rather untidy. The point is, he could've saved all that trouble, prevented unnecessary unsightliness of his machines and reduced the national tape usage index by more than four per cent if he'd just taken the time to route his cables properly.

Gear and brake cables carry out their respective tasks more efficiently if the route they take is as direct as possible, without too many detours, which create more friction with each tight bend and centimetre of distance the cable travels; instant action is required and expected from both the gear and brake cables and that means the shortest, smoothest route from lever to end.

The best way to keep the gear cables in a nice arc to the stops at the front of the frame is to use the crossover method. Right-hand gear cable goes to left-hand frame stop and vice versa. The inner wires cross each other under the down tube and continue on their designated paths to derailleur land. Some question whether the cables will rub through each other where they intersect. Well, I ask you this; have you ever taken a wire inner cable and tried to file through it? They're sturdy little bastards designed for withstanding constant rubbing; you'll be OK, at least until the next cable replacement (you do replace your cables at least once a year, don't you?) If you are bothered by the vibration when bouncing over the cobbles, just pop a couple of those little rubber grommets on the cables to keep them off the down tube and rattling their tinkling tune.

RULE #74 //
V METERS OR SMALL COMPUTERS ONLY

Forego the data and ride on feel; little compares to the pleasure of riding as hard as your mind will allow. If you are not a pro or aspiring to be one, then you don't need a power meter or heart-rate monitor. As for GPS, how often do you get lost on a ride? They are bulky, ugly and superfluous. Any cycle computer, if deemed necessary, should be simple, small and mounted on the stem. And preferably wireless.

Unfortunately, the let's-put-a-lower-case-'i'-in-front-of-every-word-to-denote-shit-you-need trend has crept into Cycling as well as everything else in life. We can now buy an actual mounting bracket to hold the 'necessary' iPhone – as if anything, least of all your social life, was more sacred than the ride itself. It is at this point that the Velominati draw the line. Anyone who stops a ride and forces others to as well so they can reply to a text message should be set upon and beaten with mini-pumps on the spot.

It all started in the 80s when the first cyclo-computers were seen. They weren't too offensive or obtrusive, except maybe for the length of wire you had to wrap round the brake cable to keep it tidy (or just left flopping around if you were a genuinely slovenly person). They told you how fast you were going, how far you'd gone and how long it took you to get there. Simple info and really all you needed.

Then someone decided that more information meant more Awesome, and that we actually needed to know how fast our legs were making circles: the cadence function was born. Totally useless, but seen still today as something that might help one become a better rider. It doesn't, it just adds to the confusion. The important thing is to move your legs as quickly as makes sense for your physiology, and your cadence device won't tell you that bit. Not to mention that the extra couple metres of wiring needed to reach the chainstay makes them even uglier and more error-prone than before.

If you're thinking your wireless set-up absolves you from this problem, think again. That wireless sensor is obnoxious in its enormity and it takes batteries, which will run out, a fact that you'll only discover after stopping to 'fix' the sensor's position – and likely make your pals wait while you do. But at least you could do all this without the mass of wires.

Of course, if you need to know how fast your legs were spinning, you'd better have data on how fast your heart is beating, too. Match the figures to each other to calculate the amount of effort put out to the amount of speed. Then take the square root of that number and run it through some differential calculus to approximate power and endurance, carry the 1 and round to the nearest number you can understand, and guess what? You still suck. Now log on to Strava and make it public.

The Prophet didn't ride with a computer, mainly because they weren't invented, granted, but all he needed to know was how much more pain he could endure as he crushed the opposition. He could feel it. If it's hurting and you're not getting anywhere, you need to hurt a bit more. There's only one number you need to know, and a computer or power meter or heart-rate monitor isn't going to tell you. The only number that matters is the number that tells you if you can go just a little bit harder. And, unless you're passing out, the answer is, predictably, yes.

A V-Meter is built into each and every one of us. How fast are you going? V. How far have you gone? V. How much power are you putting out? V.

Rip that laptop off your bars and say it again. V.

RULE #75 //
RACE NUMBERS ARE
FOR RACES

Remove it from your frame before the next training ride because no matter how cool you think it looks, it does not look cool. Unless you are in a race. In which case it looks cool.

I saw you today, but you didn't see me. I was walking down Main Road and you were at the traffic lights directly across the intersection. Your kit was immaculately matched, predominantly black with white shoes and helmet, smooth guns glistening in the sun, your bike clean and sleek. The way you unclipped and almost simultaneously positioned yourself astride the top tube was a masterclass in Casually Deliberate. I wasn't the only one to notice; the eyes of the smartly dressed women also waiting to cross the street were certainly drawn towards you, an aesthetic marvel with a Magnificent Stroke.

So why were they sniggering behind perfectly manicured hands, muttering derisive nothings to each other?

Because your number from that race three weeks ago was still stuck to your helmet, genius. No wonder you are single. How can anyone, even those who know nothing of Cycling yet a little about Looking Fantastic, take you seriously? You are the reason motorists hate us. There is nothing to be gained from riding around town with '437' taped across your noggin except scorn.

Are you that person? Liberate your helmet from the number immediately after crossing the line, before it's too late. The same goes for that flash number on your frame – tear it off. And you can get rid of that timing thing on your fork while you're at it; it didn't help in the race and it ain't helping now.

PART IV:
The Aesthete

Life can be approached in three ways.

First is the Right Way. This method is largely academic and involves specifics, instruction, study and discipline. Mostly, it involves a lot of theory provided by individuals who aren't particularly good at following their own instruction.

Second is the Wrong Way. This requires almost no academics whatsoever and is much more fun, with the specifics of the matter usually discovered empirically. In practice, we commonly refer to this particular process as 'experience'.

Third, there is the Way We Actually Do Things. This involves a combination of the first two and determines our individual style and personality. It lives between light and dark, day and night. It is on the boundary between two forms where everything interesting in life happens.

As we wrap ourselves in the fabric of Cycling, we are faced with the enormity and complexity of our chosen way of life. The suffering we experience as we strive to become better riders; the Stockholm Syndrome effect of our love for the machine that in turn causes us such comprehensive pain. We face the merciless and temperamental nature of the Man with the Hammer, and the seductive lure of his spouse, whom we know only as La Volupté. The Man with the Hammer is a hard taskmaster indeed; you will know when you meet him, or when his arrival is imminent. He comes to visit four or more hours into a hard ride, when you are depleted, after you have been drawn in and seduced by La Volupté, her soft touch caressing you when your pedal stroke is still sublime, smooth and powerful. She lures you in to a false sense of comfort – a belief that your form will last the day. And then, from out of nowhere you are struck like a hapless nail, over and over again. By this time it's usually too late to fight back, so you attempt to limit the ferocity of his blows by forcing as much solid and liquid sustenance down your gullet as you can. But he knows you are at his mercy. Once he has your body, then too shall he take your soul.

A Cycling Disciple exudes an air of confidence and a familiarity with their craft. Their kit is arranged precisely, their machines immaculate. Theirs is a refined appearance communicated through details: helmet positioned just right, the grippers of their shorts at precisely the same height round their thighs, the arms of their eyewear placed deliberately over the helmet straps.

Should their kit or machine become dirty, it will be at the end of a long, tough day in the saddle riding in cold, pouring rain – a day devoted to the hard labour of our chosen calling. Prior to hostilities, our appearance is carefully curated; yet once the hammer is dropped and the ride has begun, any concern about appearance falls by the wayside as Rule #5 takes precedence over all else.

This is a delicate art rife with paradox and enigma. Aesthetics in a sport as difficult as Cycling is itself a contradiction; surely anything wrought with such suffering should be driven The Right Way – purely by function, by practicalities, in a ruthless quest to wring every last drop of precious V from our organism in the quest to maximise performance.

Paradoxically, Cyclists are at once some of the hardest people in sport and also some of the most vain. A Cyclist knows better than perhaps any other athlete that Morale is a fickle beast that lives upon a knife's edge. It can elevate us to incredible heights yet squash us like an insect for little more than finding a spot of grime on a freshly laundered jersey or dirt on the bar tape. In order for us to ride well, we must have good Morale. In order to have good Morale, we must Look Fantastic At All Times.

The argument could be made that the best way to improve your riding is to meditate extensively on Rule #5; some even suggest that aesthetics dilute its purity. On the surface, that may be a seductive thing to believe, but it ignores the single most important fact of Cycling: Looking Fantastic is the best aphrodisiac available.

Rain falls outside my window presently, and the forecast suggests it might snow this afternoon. I face over six hours on the bike today, yet I am not deterred. As the sun lifts itself over the horizon and its dissipated light filters through the clouds and onto the streets, I climb aboard my machine dressed in my Flandrian Best of knee-warmers, woollen overshoes, jersey, gilet and a cap beneath the helmet. As rain penetrates my clothing and a bitter chill sets in, my eyes cast down to my legs as they piston along. Drops of rain fall from the brim of my cap, tapping out a rhythm. My mind fills with visions of the great Flemish races and their protagonists: Van Looy, De Vlaeminck, Merckx, Museeuw, Boonen. Any discomfort is washed away as I imagine myself suffering as they suffered. Cold is replaced by resolve, and I go on. *'The trick, William Potter, is not minding that it hurts.'* Even though the pain in my legs and lungs is searing, to all outside observers I still look immaculate, in control, my outward appearance belying the hurt that burns deep inside me. This is the modus operandi of The Aesthete.

RULE #7 //
TAN LINES
SHOULD BE CULTIVATED AND KEPT RAZOR SHARP

Under no circumstances should one roll up one's sleeves or shorts in an effort to somehow diminish one's tan lines. Sleeveless jerseys are under no circumstances to be employed.

'You must be a truck driver.'

I was cold chillin' poolside at the Luxor on the Las Vegas strip. I'm not sure what I expected her to think I was, but 'truck driver' wasn't very high on the list of possibilities.

The fact was, I was what I have always have been – a Cyclist – and my tan lines and shaved legs should make that fact plain enough. Yes, I ply my craft on wheels, two rather than eighteen. Yes, I may seem alien to 'normal' people. And no, it matters not when they turn and walk away, possibly more baffled than when they made first contact. As it happened in this particular case, her expression mixed bemusement, amusement and dismissal, and I expected no more or less.

Proper Cycling kit is designed to be tight-fitting. It should not move from its correct position. The legs of our bib shorts are lined with grippers and the arms of our jerseys with elastic cuffs. During the countless hours we spend labouring upon our machines, the sun will beat down upon us, imprinting our legs and arms with distinct tan lines, generally considered to be fashionably distasteful for a reason whose justification baffles and eludes me.

There are two ways of approaching this aspect of La Vie Velominatus.* First, you can worry about the fact that our tight clothing creates tan lines, and consider any number of doomed tactics to limit how obvious they are, all of which will serve only to exacerbate the problem. You can then turn to more desperate measures involving wearing clothing that attempts to conceal them when in social settings, all as convincing as Granny Olive's jet-black dyed hair or Uncle Harold's mismatched and askew toupé.

Or, you can embrace it as a mark of the ilk. A tribal marking of a dedicated Cyclist who takes care to wear their kit properly and positioned in precisely the same location for each and every ride. We bear the marks of our dedication to The Work proudly – shaved legs, crash scars and all. Of these marks, our razor-sharp tan lines stand on the front line.

*There exists a third option, which is to wear baggy clothing instead of proper Cycling kit. We disregard this notion in its entirety on the basis that we are not savages.

RULE #14 //
SHORTS SHOULD BE
BLACK

Team-issue shorts should be black, with the possible exception of side panels, which may match the rest of the team kit.

Professionals wear what their team requires, like it or not. We civilians have the luxury of choice – maybe *too many* choices, as it turns out – so we look to Rule #14 for guidance.

Simply put, shorts should be black. They may have a panel on the sides that matches the team kit, but nothing more. They can *never* be all white. Wet, dirty, white Lycra is basically transparent; enough said on that matter.

Looking Fantastic on the bike is the whole point. As you climb, as you suffer, as you descend, as you blow through a small town centre. Having something other than black shorts is a visual distraction that no one needs. Why so conservative, you ask – can't I rock these fantastic green bibs that Thor wore when he rode for French team Crédit Agricole? In a word, no, because frankly, it never ends. Lycra can be sublimated with endless colours and designs. The genie is already out of the bottle and we need to stuff his hot-pink Lycra-wearing ass back in.

In the halcyon days of racing, shorts were always black wool. Coppi, Bartali and Gimondi never showed up in natural-coloured (i.e. white) wool shorts. Everyone had a drawer full of black wool shorts with a real leather chamois sewn in. Eventually some letters were sewn on, a little advertising, but that was all: it never got out of hand, no free-for-all, no one lost an eye.

Black hides dirt and grease. It looks great and it doesn't distract the eye from the massive shaved leg. Grab a clean pair and move on. They're like the little black cocktail dress: they go with everything. When wool was overrun by black slick Lycra for shorts in the 80s, it was an exciting development. Some of the early Lycra was glossy and smooth. Everyone (except maybe Sean Kelly) saw the smooth, glossy early Lycra as an improvement – the crude leather chamois was still there – but visually things were great. Someone always has to stir the pot, though, and this time it was Nalini, the kit maker for Miguel Indurain's Banesto team. They made a kit of dark blue rather than black. While purists deemed this an outrage on the scale of the Pope wearing a gold speedo for Sunday Mass, actually it looked rather sharp. Another development was the invention of sublimation of colour into the Lycra: jerseys and side panels on shorts were now rolling bill-boards for as much advertising as a sponsor was willing to pay for. Carrera Jeans cleverly came up with Lycra shorts that looked like faded blue cotton denim. There was disorder in the house.

Thankfully, with the demise of the Carrera team, faux denim was never seen again in the peloton, yet all manner of other gaudy designs and colours replaced it. Still, this is no reason for the non-sponsored pro rider, i.e. the rest of us, to imitate these offensively garish rolling billboards. Go black, and never go back.

RULE #15 //

BLACK SHORTS SHOULD ALSO BE WORN WITH LEADER'S JERSEYS

Black shorts, or at least standard team-kit shorts, must be worn with Championship jerseys and race leadership jerseys. Don't over-match your kit – or over-match and accept that you will look like a douche.

A casual reading of Rule #15 would suggest that we are lecturing the professionals on their dress code. Yes, that would be correct.

This is The Right Way.

There's no such term as the leader's bib shorts or the leader's socks; it's just the leader's *jersey*. The only way to complement such a prestigious jersey is to wear black shorts – or be Mario Cipollini.

Pros exhibit a tendency to match the shorts (and more) to the jersey for maximum effect. Some might say the Italians exemplify this, and with Mario Cipollini, the most macho and photogenic Italian Cyclist ever, they would have a strong example. Super Mario won the World Championship road race in 2002 and for the ensuing year every bit of

Normally, this would be The Wrong Way.

his kit, from helmet down to shoes, was *white* with rainbow stripes. Normally this would be a problem. For Mario it would be a problem if everything was *not so*.

Cipo had finally won Milan–Sanremo earlier in the year, so adding a World Championship to his palmarès was perhaps the crowning glory of his career. The motor racing course in Zolder, Belgium was flat and wide open, designed for a sprint finish. The Italian national team was all-in for Cipo, an unusual occurrence in itself as on more than one occasion they had been known for working against each other. But in Zolder the money was all on Mario, and it paid off.

Finally as World Champion, we knew he was going to celebrate as only he could: everything white, everything rainbow striped. Being tall, handsome, super-fast on a bike and Italian, Cipo was willing and able to pull off stunts no one else could. He ran up a steady tally of Swiss Franc fines flouting the UCI's rules on team clothing being predominantly based on the *actual* team clothing!

For Cipo, Grand Tour prologues were a chance to wear neck-to-ankle skinsuits of outrageous designs. He cut the sleeves off his jersey on hot days. He said nice things about his Cannondale bike to the TV motos. What a pro.

So how does Rule #15 affect the civilian? The chances any of us are going to be in a leader's jersey are slim to none. As such, your best opportunity to invoke Rule #15 is when casually reading your copy of *La Gazzetta Dello Sport* at an outdoor café in Milan. Upon seeing the Giro's points leader in a complete Maglia Ciclamino mauve helmet-to-sock kit, one mutters 'Madonna, Rule #15 per favoré,' then throws the pink paper in the air for the waiter to pick up, leaves the table and casually walks off along the promenade.

RULE #16 //
RESPECT
THE JERSEY

Championship and race-leader jerseys must only be worn if you've won the championship or led the race.

It doesn't matter how good you think you look in that leader's jersey. It's not this good.

Greg 'LeMan' is simply that. You are simply not. Take cues from him, but realise you can never pull this off. Do not attempt.

The most coveted jerseys in Cycling transcend any of the men and women who have worn them. They represent the most noble attributes of the sport: dedication, skill, perseverance, strength. Elements we espouse more frequently than we attain. Attributes the Italians aptly call *grinta* and the French refer to as *panache*. The *Maillot Jaune* of the Tour de France reflects these ideals at the highest level of not just our sport, but any. The Rainbow Jersey symbolises *grinta* and *panache* for the rider who represented their country in victory over the best riders from all Cycling nations of the world. The *Maglia Rosa* is presented to the rider who is the strongest over a three-week period on the most savage and beautiful roads Cycling has ever known. The Dotty Jumper is reserved for the best climber over the highest mountain roads in the sport.

In order to compete for one of these jerseys, one has to be part of an elite class of athlete, a clique only joined by the naturally gifted. In a Grand Tour, this upper echelon consists of ten riders at best and realistically just three. The World Championship road race, being a one-day event, may be contested by more riders than a Grand Tour, which serves to make it even more competitive in terms of the depth of the field contesting the win. Couple this fierce competition with a course that is over 250km long and it is no wonder that the winner of the rainbow bands is permitted to wear the jersey for an entire year and may adorn their kit with the bands for the rest of their career. In order to win one of these jerseys you need a mysterious combination of perfect form, a suitable course, a team willing to support you and often a bit of luck. Moreover, you need generous helpings of *grinta* and *panache*.

Rule #16, then, is all about Reverence. Take a moment to

recall the images of the riders over the years wearing champion and leader's jerseys. Now think of the names of those who've earned those jerseys. Chances are, if you're reading this book, you did not imagine yourself or invoke your own name. (If you did think of your own name, please autograph your copy of this book and send it along to The Keepers c/o Velominati World Headquarters). Granted, you ride hard and lay down The V at every opportunity. Maybe you even think you can sprint like Cipo, time-trial like Faboo or climb like Il Pirata. Remember this though: you can't. And even if you could, you couldn't do it in the heat of competition in the biggest arenas of Cycling. So unless you've bested the best at the Worlds, ridden onto the Champs Elysees in yellow or wooed the tifosi wearing pink in Milan, you have absolutely no business wearing the jerseys that say you did.

In recent years, some of the names that have worn the most sacred garments in Cycling have been besmirched by scandal. This has led to some of these jerseys being passed from one dubious champion to the next long after the race has ended and been entered into the history books. Debates have been won, lost and mostly gone unresolved as we spilled beer in arguments over the merits of rider X, governing body Y and testing protocol Z. At the heart of these arguments are the misgivings and indiscretions of those responsible for their stewardship. We need to be clear here: a Velominatus may question the motives of the rider, but never do they question the integrity of the jersey. The sacredness of these jerseys and what they represent is as pure as a hand-brazed Italian frame. The only difference is you *can* go out and ride a hand-brazed frame.

RULE #17 //
TEAM KIT IS
FOR MEMBERS OF
THE TEAM

Wearing pro team kit is also questionable if you're not paid to wear it. If you must fly the colours of pro teams, all garments should match perfectly, i.e no Mapei jersey with Kelme shorts and Telekom socks.

Admittedly, this is more of a guideline than a Rule. After all, it states 'questionable' and who among us hasn't thrown down for some team kit at one point or another? Therein lies the rub. Typically, when a rider picks up team kit it is in the form of a jersey, maybe some socks or, even more typically, a cap. Total commitment to matching bib shorts and arm- and knee-warmers, not to mention gloves and shoe covers, is rare. So when in doubt fly your V-kit, club strip or other non-team matching kit and get on with it.

A special dispensation is also considered for 'throwback' jerseys. Sporting the likes of a La Vie Claire or Team Z jersey on occasion demonstrates your knowledge of the teams of old and the nostalgic times of toe clips, hairnets and round frame tubes. When donning the classic jersey, however, consider these four things: 1) If you don't have matching team shorts then they must be solid black. 2) You had better be prepared to discuss team specifics such as riders and wins. If you don't know that Big Mig rode for Banesto from '90–'96 and won all five of his Tours as well as two Giro–Tour doubles in that kit, you'd be well advised to leave it at home. 3) It's preferable to wear said jersey while riding a classic steel and/or period-appropriate bike. 4) If you're rocking a Molteni jersey, it had better be wool and on Festum Prophetae (Eddy Merckx's birthday).

RULE #18 //
KNOW WHAT TO WEAR.
DON'T SUFFER
KIT CONFUSION

No baggy shorts or jerseys while riding the road bike. No lycra when riding the mountain bike (unless racing XC). Skin suits only for cyclocross and time trials.

It's one of the great misdemeanours of modern society: the 4WD or SUV, being put to use in totally inappropriate ways. Soccer moms driving the kids to school, then off to the supermarket before lunch with the girls and a quick afternoon dalliance with the pool guy before retrieving the little darlings from the Montessori. While this sounds like a tough day for the manicured middle-aged set, the lack of muddy bogs, steep, rutted driveways and sand dunes renders the big, ungainly vehicles impractical at best and pointless at worst.

Like the 4WD, mountain bikes were invented with only one purpose in mind: to ride off-road. The early examples may have just been beefed-up old beach cruisers, or klunkers, but the pioneers who cobbled them together took their inspiration from the motocross set and utilised fat tyres with traction-giving knobs; wide, straight handlebars with no drops; big cushy saddles and inefficient, heavy drum brakes. The bikes may not have worked very well, but there was no doubting their intended use. And when the bearded riders wanted to ride on the road, well, they used their road bikes. There really was no middle ground.

As the mountain bike evolved, a lot of road bike technology (if you could call it that, as innovation wasn't exactly leaping forward in the skinny-tyre world) crept over to the dirt. We wanted lighter frames and wheels so we could climb steep hills more easily, while not compromising strength. Racing was initially done downhill, before cross-country came to be the dominant form of competition. A lot of road riders made the crossover, bringing with them supreme fitness but not much in the way of bike-handling skills. They also brought their impractical clothing. Lycra shorts and light-weight, clinging jerseys were perfect for the road, but crash in the dirt in that get-up and you were going to come out like a plum in a sock that had been put through a blender.

With the long-travel mountain bikes that are prominent today sporting an increased ability to crush any terrain, having a skinny, shaved-legged, heart-rate monitor-wearing dweeb in Lycra perched atop 29-inch wheels is simply *wrong*. Stick some baggy shorts and a loose-fitting, long-sleeved top on them and you instantly have a mountain biker. Long-fingered gloves and a peaked, rounded profile helmet are an integral part of the dirt rider's aesthetic; it all just fits. Then, when you inevitably go sliding down the trail on your hip or are launched headfirst into the under-growth, you can thank your Lycra-clad predecessors who at least did you an honourable service by volunteering themselves as early crash-test dummies. It's the least they could have done.

RULE #19 //
INTRODUCE YOURSELF

If you deem it appropriate to join a group of riders who are not part of an open group ride and who are not your mates, it is customary and courteous to announce your presence. Introduce yourself and ask if you may join the group. If you have been passed by a group, wait for an invitation, introduce yourself or let them go. The silent joiner is viewed as ill-mannered and Anti-V. Conversely, the joiner who can't shut their cakehole is no better and should be dropped from the group at first opportunity.

Imagine this scene for a moment: it's your father's birthday, and you and your family have arranged a special celebratory dinner at a nice restaurant. Nothing over the top or too extravagant, just a relaxed atmosphere, good food and reasonable prices. You have been here before, the staff know you and in the course of the evening you bump into some friends and colleagues also enjoying the establishment this evening. The ambience of the room is not too loud, and you can hold a proper conversation without having to speak in hushed tones. It's civil.

As are you. Halfway through your entrée, you notice a lone patron enter the premises. You don't take much further notice and continue to enjoy your meal. The wine is flowing and everyone is relaxed, having a good time. You excuse yourself and retreat to the facilities to freshen up. On return, you are surprised, even shocked, to see that the guy you noticed earlier has pulled up a chair next to yours. He tucks into his meal and helps himself to the bottle of Merlot. Your family sits in stunned silence, not knowing where to look or what to say. You ask your father if he knows this intruder, and he responds in the negative. He just sat down and started eating and drinking, not saying a word, you are told. You politely yet firmly ask him to leave, and without any words or emotion, he is gone.

It's unlikely that this would ever happen, right? And you certainly wouldn't be the fellow who makes himself at home at a table full of random diners. So why is it that some Cyclists think it is perfectly acceptable to jump on in to someone else's bunch ride, or tack onto the wheel of another rider and feast at the veritable Cycling dining table?

We are not savages, and if you are out on a solo ride, suffering into a block headwind, and happen upon another rider or group doing the same, then both parties should be willing to help each other out; the group could use an extra helper, and the solo rider can take some respite from their solitary suffering. The group should extend an invitation, or the soloist offer an introduction and humbly request that they join. It's what separates us from the unsociable outcasts of society and football fans.

RULE #21 //
COLD WEATHER GEAR IS FOR COLD WEATHER

Knickers, vests, arm-warmers, shoe covers and caps beneath your helmet can all make you look like a hardman, when the weather warrants their use.

Dark clouds loom over the pavé of Paris-Roubaix.

'The thing about the cold is that you can never tell how cold it is from looking out a kitchen window. You have to dress up, get out training and when you come back, you then know how cold it is.'

Sean Kelly

Cycling, in essence, is a minimalist's endeavour. We look at ways to shave mere grams from our bikes to unburden ourselves from unnecessary accoutrement. We are careful to replace only the calories we burn so that we might climb a little faster. We take only what we need to repair common mechanicals on the road and tend to wonder if we really need even that. So it stands to reason that we do not turn up for a fair-weather ride dressed in our Flandrian Best.

Selection of appropriate Cycling attire can be tricky, especially in the shoulder seasons or on days with wild swings in the weather. For these reasons, cold-weather gear was developed to be versatile. Arm- and knee-warmers can easily be slipped off and stowed in a jersey pocket when the roads dry out and temperatures rise. A quality rain cape can be used to repel driving rain as well as biting wind. But perhaps the most useful piece in the Velominatus' foul-weather kit is a properly sized gilet.

The utility of the gilet is nearly impossible to overstate. Its main function is to keep the Cyclist's core warm by adding a thin membrane over the jersey that traps heat and blocks wind. In application, however, the gilet exceeds its designed performance envelope and serves as an apt water-repelling insulation layer. If one were to accidentally leave anything out of one's cold-weather bag, one would hope it wasn't the gilet. An additional word of advice here is to *start cold* in anticipation of warming up on your ride. Yes, it can be tempting to roll out looking pro, replete in your woolen knee- and arm-warmers, but when you do you'd better be anticipating grey skies, wet roads and perhaps some mud, wind and snow.

RULE #22 //
CYCLING CAPS ARE FOR CYCLING

Cycling caps can be worn under helmets, but never when not riding, no matter how hip you think you look. This will render one a douche, and should result in public berating or beating. The only time it is acceptable to wear a Cycling cap is while directly engaged in Cycling activities and while clad in Cycling kit. This includes activities taking place prior to and immediately after the ride such as machine-tuning and tyre-pumping. Also included are café appearances for pre-ride espressi and post-ride pub appearances for body-refuelling ales (provided said pub has sunny, outdoor patio – do not stray inside a pub wearing kit or risk being ceremoniously beaten by leather-clad biker chicks).

Under these conditions, having your cap skull-side tipped jauntily at a rakish angle is, one might say, de rigueur. All good things must be taken in measure, however, and as such it is critical that we let sanity and good taste prevail: as long as the first sip of the relevant caffeine or hop-based beverage is taken whilst beads of sweat, snow or rain are still evident on one's brow then it is legitimate for the cap to be worn. However, once all that remains in the cranial furrows is salt, it is then time to shower and throw on some suitable après-ride attire. A woollen T.I. Raleigh training top circa '73 comes to mind.

While the cigar is perhaps frowned upon in our modern era, the wearing of the cap in this instance is *de rigeur*.

Perhaps no other accessory in the Cyclist's kit is more recognisable to the uninitiated than the Cycling cap. The cap epitomises the Velominatus as much as shaved legs, Lycra and tan lines. Classic short-brimmed cotton caps are elegant and were primarily made to be worn alone, but also to fit seamlessly underneath one's helmet. Wearing a cap has long been the après-ride headwear of choice for representing sponsors on the podium while at the same time looking good for the public and maybe a podium girl or two. Although not advisable, wearing a cap sans helmet is a long-practised custom on winter training rides.

Once the Disciple attempts to rationalise the wearing of a cap when *not* engaged in Cycling-related activities, then the slope becomes ever more slippery. There are many excuses that are made in favour of donning a cap *off-bike*. They are a simple way of identifying with and taking pride in being a Cyclist. Caps can be had inexpensively, thus making them easy to collect. Jerseys, on the other hand, would put a sizeable dent in the wallet if one were to go overboard with their collection. A rich cache of new, as well as throwback, team caps demonstrates one's understanding of and reverence for our sport. It goes without saying that wearing a jersey or, Merckx forbid, shorts, is forbidden for non-Cycling related activities, yet one may ask what harm there is in wearing a simple cap. With so many apparently plausible reasons to sport a Cycling cap when not Cycling, it almost seems ludicrous to have a Rule on the matter.

Adding to the complications of obeying Rule #22 are two additional factors. Alarmingly, Pros seem to be replacing the Cycling cap with a baseball-style hat. The once de rigueur Cycling cap worn to sign-ins and on podiums of pro races is increasingly being replaced by what amounts to nothing more than a NASCAR-style, large-billed abomination.

Hipsters and other Johnny-come-lately Cyclists are quick to adopt the cap as a coming-out type of statement to their new-found life as a Cyclist. These people will plop a Molteni cap on their heads without as much as an inkling of who The Prophet is, or for that matter, a passing interest in Rule #9 riding. For these two reasons alone, the Cycling cap needs to be reclaimed by the Velominati and restored to its rightful position in Cycling aesthetics and tradition.

Once again, the allure of disobedience to Rule #22 is a test of your faith in leading the life of the Cycling Disciple. If you choose to break this Rule, however, let the righteous indignation of impunity wash over you. Bathe in the light of the others who have brazenly, and without remorse, worn their 7-Eleven, Peugeot or Telekom caps to cafés and pubs the world over.

Like any heretic spitting in the face of conformity, do your level best in swaying the hearts and minds of the sheep who question nothing and follow blindly. For if wearing a Cycling cap is your cross to bear, it is also yours to reclaim for those who have gone before us and those who will come after.

RULE #23 //
TUCK ONLY AFTER REACHING
ESCAPE VELOCITY

You may only employ the aerodynamic tuck after you have spun out your top gear. Your legs make you go fast, and trying to keep your fat ass out of the wind only serves to keep you from slowing down once you reach escape velocity. Thus, the tuck is to be employed only to prevent you slowing down when your legs have wrung the top end out of your block. Tucking prematurely while descending is the antithesis of Casually Deliberate. For more on riding fast downhill see Rule #64 and Rule #85.

The aerodynamic tuck is the hallmark of the Casually Deliberate rider. Sean Yates hanging his shoulders over the bars with his chin nearly resting on his front tyre; Paulo Bettini tucking his tiny form into the area between his saddle and top tube; Greg LeMond dangling his rear end high off the back of his saddle and getting his shoulders as low as possible. These are some of the greatest shows of defiance in Cycling; the racer has accelerated to the point where the pedals become useless, yet they persist in their effort to go faster still.

There are some who ride among us, however, who believe the tuck is a handy tool any time the road points downhill. Not true: the tuck is a great way to go fast when there is no more fast to be found in the drive train. Tucking when one can still pedal is a great way to go slow while looking like an idiot. For those interested in that line of work, I recommend unicycles and recumbents.

Note the position of LeMond's chain. *Allez le douze.*

RULE #27 //
SHORTS AND SOCKS SHOULD BE LIKE GOLDILOCKS

Not too long and not too short. (Disclaimer: despite Sean Yates's horrible choice in shorts length, he is a quintessential hardman of Cycling and is deeply admired by the Velominati. Whereas Armstrong's short and sock lengths were just plain wrong.) No socks is a no-no, as are those ankle-length ones that should be worn only by female tennis players.

There is a fine line between Looking Fantastic and Looking Idiotic. As it specifically relates to Cycling, socks cannot be too tall or short and shorts cannot be too short or long. Track riders get an exemption and for some reason don't have to wear socks at all, but for everyone else, a 5 to 12 centimetre cuff as measured from the ankle to the top of the cuff is the accepted benchmark.

Cycling shorts only come in two lengths: men's and women's. Female Cyclists' legs Look Fantastic and covering them with more Lycra is unnecessary. Fellas, unless your name starts with Tommy and ends in Voeckler, don't you be wearing women's bib shorts just to show more thigh. Come to think of it, if your name *is* Tommy V, stop wearing women's bib shorts.

Socks, specifically ankle socks or way-too-tall socks, are a problem that cannot be tolerated. Armstrong started this mess because he liked to buck tradition. Upending tradition is all good and well if something better is resultant, but his offerings were way-too-tall black socks (see Rule #28).

His shorts, on the other hand, were lucky to be even *called* shorts, such was their extreme length. More like short knickers. Either way, totally unacceptable. They were a visual affront to the guns. We work so hard at honing them, why would you cover them up?

The length of shorts and socks is specified to complement the Cyclist's legs. The legs are our tools of the trade, and if they don't look good (see Rule #33), you're doomed. Rule #27 is to ensure your guns are framed in the best possible manner.

Wiggins and Armstrong are two riders opposite in most ways, yet they share the same length issues. Both favour the way-too-tall sock but at least Wiggo's socks are not always black. We are not playing basketball here. Tube socks stay on the court. The cuff should come to just above or below the narrowest point between the ankle bone and the calf. To be clear, no way should socks get anywhere *near* the calf muscle. If you have short, stumpy legs, then your shorts and socks should be kept as short as allowable; you don't want to make short legs look even shorter by increasing the amount of material on them. If you have long, slim legs, then a touch more length can be a good thing to make them look less like Boom's. Wiggo is the perfect example of a bad thing though. DO NOT follow his lead.

If you require visual examples, it is simple. Look at every rider from Miguel Indurain back: tanned shaven legs, socks not too high, never too low, shorts just right.

Le Professeur explains Rule #27.

RULE #28 //
SOCKS CAN BE ANY DAMN
COLOUR YOU LIKE

White is old-school cool. Black is cool too, but was given a bad image by a Texan whose socks were too long. If you feel you must go coloured, make sure they damn well match your kit.

And by 'any colour' we mean white. In a perfect world, beautiful Italian wool/silk blend Cycling socks would still be readily available. They would be all white, maybe a nice stripe of colour at the cuff. But we now live in the dark ages of Cycling socks. The world will look back on this time and wonder how we survived, how we got through to the end of it all.

Is a shaved head better than a mullet? Is a horrible, thick, prolific, baleen-like eastern European 'tache better than the ubiquitous Seattle goatee? Who can say? Since when did walking through airports with a neck-support cushion already in the deployed position seem acceptable? The point is, we have lost our azimuth on the great sphere of style. What does this have to do with Rule #28? Not much besides the Dark Ages argument.

One can't find really nice completely white Cycling socks, so the best one can hope for is *mostly* white Cycling socks. Grey socks, yellow socks, pink socks: sure, socks can be any damn colour you please, but let's get a grip. White is the obvious choice for the Velominatus.

Many cowards argue that only non-white socks are acceptable for wet, dirty conditions as the socks are going to end up dirty and grimy. Of course they would be wrong. Do cricketers start off wearing grass-stained grey uniforms? One starts the ride looking the tits, and there is no excuse for doing otherwise. If one ends up with black grimy socks that's great too, as Rule #9 has been observed. One does not start with dark socks or a dirty kit because it's going to get nasty out there. Rule #9 riding with booties where the socks are covered up is a bad excuse. Covered up until the emergency room tech is cutting off your booties with those badass scissors. Then they realize the drapes don't match the douche. 'Look what we have here, little mister Euro-Pro fell off his bike. Now he is in the ER and we all know his dirty little secret. He uses his booties to cover up his black socks.'

The same visual aids from Rule #27 can be used here. Look at Indurain, Merckx, Coppi, Kelly. Every single rider is wearing white socks. They didn't wear red socks on training days, or grey socks when it was snowing or blue socks if they were having a 'does my ass look big in these tights' day.

This Rule pertains to road Cycling. No one cares what one wears on a mountain bike or cyclo-cross bike.

RULE #31 //
SPARE TUBES, MULTI-TOOLS AND REPAIR KITS SHOULD BE STORED IN JERSEY POCKETS

If absolutely necessary, in a converted bidon in a cage on bike.

Rule #31 might be viewed as closing the loophole left agape by Rule #29. For if you're left with no saddlebag you shouldn't be thinking it is OK to go out and buy a bar bag, frame bag or, Merckx forbid, wear some sort of back pack. Of course the workaround to Rule #29 here is the converted bidon. An old bidon stuffed with tyre repair and other road-side do-it-yourself paraphernalia can be quite an elegant problem-solver for the overstuffed-jersey weary. Beware though – it comes at the risk of becoming dehydrated and being less self-reliant out on the road. This is probably best reserved for shorter rides and/or those with ample water access.

RULE #32 //
HUMPS ARE FOR CAMELS:
NO HYDRATION PACKS

Hydration packs are never to be seen on a road rider's body. No argument will be entered into on this. For MTB and long-distance gravel riding, they are cool.

Marko bridges up to the lead group at the 2012 Heck of the North. As in, Heck Yes, he's wearing a camelbak.

Although it states it right there in the subtext, some still want to argue. Well, one that I know of. And I don't even know if this serial violator of, and indeed inspiration for, The Rules still practises this dangerous art. Maybe he's moved on; bought the kit, ditched the hump. We can only hope.

There are only so many times you can tell someone before you get bored with it, even if they themselves don't seem to be. Their continued resistance can wear you down, and their case is inevitably closed and filed under 'too hard', 'lost cause'. But like a petty thief who has spent too much time in and out of court and prison being 'rehabilitated', the serial violator keeps turning up for rides seemingly oblivious to the warnings administered to them, virtually waving their smoking gun right in your face.

Their reasons are all too familiar, and all too often based on issues of practicality. We're not Cyclists to be practical for God's sake, so you can keep your concerns about hydration and the ability to carry extra food, clothing and enough tools to do a tear-down and rebuild of the bike at the side of the road shoved way down there in the bottom of your pack, somewhere under the squashed PB&J sandwich and the BB tool held to a 12' crescent wrench by a roll of duct tape.

The fact that it's the middle of an Australian summer and 40C out is irrelevant; keep refilling your two small bidons and at least look halfway respectable as you cramp up in a salty, screaming ball at the side of the road with 35km still to go. It's worth it.

If you're riding your mountain bike or are on a remote gravel ride though, disregard everything stated. Obviously you need the camelbak to carry a bow and arrow and a club to kill your next meal. Not for extra water.

RULE #33 //
SHAVE YOUR GUNS

Legs are to be carefully shaved at all times. If, for some reason, your legs are to be left hairy, make sure you can dish out plenty of hurt to shaved riders, or be considered a hippie douche on your way to a Critical Mass. Whether you use a straight razor or a bowie knife, use Baxter to keep them smooth.

Ask any non-Disciple to play word association when you say 'Cyclist' and one of their utterances will almost undoubtedly be 'shaved legs'. Having shaved guns, after all, is one of the three dead giveaways of a Velominatus (the other two being crisp tan lines and body dysmorphia). The Velominata comes by shaved guns a little more honestly, but for male Cyclists, shaving the guns for the first time is a rite of passage into the Way of the Cycling Disciple.

The origins of Cyclists shaving their legs reach well into history, this we know. What is not as clear is the reason behind this ritual. Some say it is to improve aerodynamics. Others say riders started shaving their legs to make them smoother and more amenable for the masseur to apply embrocation. Yet another origin story, and perhaps the most compelling, is that legs were shaved to prevent hair from getting scabbed over by road rash, thus making it easier to manage wounds. Truthfully, we probably all shave our legs for no other reason than it's been passed down from one generation of Cyclists to the next. It's just what we do. It's a tribal thing; it lets others know we are Cyclists.

Shaving your legs is without doubt the single least expensive thing you can do to look pro. Next time you get the chance, compare two riders in your local group. One with shaved guns and one without and ask yourself which looks more Pro.

What's more, shaved guns can make up for a rider having decidedly less-than-Pro kit. That's how Pro shaving is. Consider riders A and B for this next example. Rider A shows up at the Saturday-afternoon group ride replete with a perfectly matched kit, a bike that looks like it was just stolen from the Europcar service course and hairy legs. Rider B rolls up with a mismatched kit, a bike that is well maintained but not 'top-shelf', and smooth, hairless cannons. Who would you think was the true Disciple? Which of the two riders' wheel would you want to follow? If you answered with 'Rider B', you are on The Path.

Inevitably, the question will be asked. Whether it be from your significant other, a co-worker or your obnoxious ball-sport-loving in-law at the family holiday get-together. Somebody will ask if and why your shave your legs. This question must be answered with the Casually Deliberate (see Rule #80) air only a Disciple can have in such matters. Under no circumstance should the merits of leg-shaving be debated with a non-Cyclist. Yes, guide the uninitiated Cyclist in their own decision to ultimately shave. But you'd have just as much success trying to explain or justify this ritual to the non-Cyclist as you would explaining rocket science to a puppy. Neither topic do you fully understand nor can you explain it to the given audience. But that doesn't mean you don't know they are true.

Finally, it has been empirically proven that how you feel about yourself impacts your performance. When you feel better, you perform better. This holds as much truth in your Cycling life as it does in your professional life. A bespoke suit from Savile Row shouldn't be something you invest in so you can impress other people. It should be something you wear to feel the best about yourself you possibly can. This self-confidence is what ultimately impresses and gives you the edge in the workplace. If it didn't we'd all be wearing sweatpants to the office. The same holds true for shaving your pins. Do this not to prove to anybody that you are a Velominatus. Do it because it will make you *feel* like a Velominatus. In so doing you will ride stronger and gain an edge over other Cyclists, even if it is only in your mind.

RULE #35 //
NO VISORS ON THE ROAD

Road helmets can be worn on mountain bikes, but never the other way round. If you want shade, see Rule #22.

Like Rule #34, this fashion disaster is cross-contamination from mountain biking. The helmet visor has its origins in motocross and enduro where deflecting tree branches away from the face is a good idea. As a road Cyclist, the only time one hopes to deflect branches away from the face is when the bike and rider have left the road and are on an uncharted course towards trouble. In that case one has one's eyes closed in fear and Cycling-specific eyewear in place (Rule #36) so no one loses an eye.

It also looks very naff and unprofessional – and hence, banned for the Velominati.

The forced transition from no helmet to hairnet, to hardshell helmet was aesthetically painful. The hairnet had a certain *je ne sais quoi* about it. It said, 'I have to wear something on my head and this won't do much but when enough of us tough boys wear them, it will be cool'. In fact, so many hardmen wore them, the hairnet is possibly the coolest headgear ever worn by a cyclist in the history of Cycling, except the Cycling Cap or just Plain old Hair.

The Gods on Mount Velomis did not smile on the early hardshell helmet. The earliest iteration (beyond ice hockey and climbing helmets) was the much unloved and yet still commonly-seen giant Bell-biker hardshell helmet. It was heavy, plastic, stupid, and pathetic in every respect.

The extremely stylish Cinelli hairnet helmet worn by the extremely tough Sean Kelly was replaced . . .

Helmets are a necessity now and most of us feel naked without one. But too much money has been spent to find any given year's best balance of aerodynamics, protection, airflow and good looks. The helmet is still basically ugly,

. . . by this Brancale attempt at a hard-shell helmet. Even Kelly winning Milan-Sanremo in this helmet could not have boosted the sales of such an ill-conceived bit of plastic.

and adding a visor to the front of it compounds the problem. Now you really look like an arse, but in order to keep our brains in our skulls, we always use helmets – period. Yes we would look better either with a properly cocked cotton cap or Sean's Cinelli hairnet, but we like our brains in the skull, thank you very much.

RULE #36 //
EYEWEAR SHALL BE CYCLING-SPECIFIC

No Aviator shades, blue-blockers or clip-on covers for eye glasses.

Take a moment to study the following list: Ottavio Bottecchia, Fausto Coppi (above), Jean Bobet, Jan Janssen, Bernard Hinault, Laurent Fignon, Martin Earley.

If your name isn't on that list and you're not riding with Cycling-specific eyewear, then you'd better take your blue-blockers down to your local bike shop right this moment and swap them for a set of proper riding shades.

RULE #37 //

THE ARMS OF THE EYEWEAR SHALL ALWAYS BE PLACED OVER THE HELMET STRAPS

Part IV: The Aesthete

202

No exceptions. This is for various reasons that may or may not matter; it's just the way it is.

Helmets have run through a bit of an evolution over the years. They started out as being leather skullcaps called 'hairnets' that served no function beyond psychological comfort something akin to overdraft protection; while the bank will cover the charge, you're still in the hole in terms of maintaining control of your faculties.

The first time I heard anyone make mention of this particular piece of kit was my father having a chat with a store clerk who appeared to be emphasizing the utility of the polycarbonate (i.e. effective) helmet. My dad was lost, arguing that many a Cyclist had done well with the leather bits holding their head in place. The proprietor of the shop – who I later discovered was insane – argued that the hairnet was effective as long as your head didn't hit anything that got between the strips of leather.

The lesson here is that just because someone is crazy doesn't mean they're wrong.

By the time I got a hold of a Cycling helmet, it weighed more than my bicycle and featured a strap system that went from my chin to the outside of the helmet just fore and aft of my ear, not unlike today's helmet.

But because the helmet was about an inch thick, this meant the strap travelled from my chin to a location about an inch from my head on the four points where the straps met the helmet, much like one might lash a crib to the deck of an aircraft carrier.

As helmet technology evolved, the strap moved closer and closer to the cranium, mostly for the fact that it looked less awkward and helped the helmet stay put in the event of a sudden and unanticipated meeting between rider and tarmac.

Today, the straps of the helmet are flush with the face of the rider; the arms of the eyewear follow the natural path from the outside of the face towards the ear – outside the strap of the helmet. When you crash, the eyewear can fly free of the helmet and not get jammed into your million-dollar face, assuming you have a face like mine. If you're ugly, we don't really care what you do; you're a lost cause already.

RULE #44 //
POSITION MATTERS

In order to find the V-Locus, a rider's handlebars on their road bike must always be lower than their saddle. The only exception to this is if you're revolutionising the sport, in which case you must also be prepared to break the World Hour Record. The minimum allowable tolerance is 4cm; there is no maximum, but people may berate you if they feel intimidated by your monster bar drop.

The reason behind lowering the handlebars is fourfold.

The most obvious is aerodynamics: lowering the bars lowers your frontal surface area, thereby allowing the rider to punch a smaller hole through the air as they draw on the power of The V to propel themselves forward.

The second reason to lower the bars is that leverage is improved, allowing the rider to make better use of their upper-body strength to load the pedals. When the bars are too high, the Racing Bicycle is transformed into a Sunday Cruiser and the power of The V vanishes.

The third reason is stability. Stability is the key to becoming comfortable on a bicycle, and the key to stability is to lower the centre of mass. Since our torsos (together with our craniums) are the heaviest chunks of our bodies (this is true for some more than others), lowering our shoulders means a significant percentage of our body weight will be brought closer to the ground, dramatically improving the stability of the bicycle/rider unit.

The first three reasons are obviously just excuses; the fourth reason is where it's at: low handlebars look the business.

The effect of this can be dramatic. I have suffered from lower back pain for the duration of my life as a Velominatus. Conventional wisdom stated that the way to ease this problem was to raise the bars and reduce the strain on my back. Yet, the more I raised the bars, the sooner my back would begin to hurt. Frustrated and desperate, I decided to move in the opposite direction and dropped my bars as far as they would go. The pain vanished.

When the bars are too high, we engage the muscles in our lower back to stabilise the bicycle. This results in thousands of small movements in response to every bump and wobble the bicycle encounters. With the centre of mass lowered, the bicycle is less susceptible to wobbles and the strain is removed from the lower back.

RULE #45 //
SLAM
YOUR STEM

A maximum stack height of 2cm is allowed below the stem and a single 5mm spacer must always – always – be stacked above. A 'slammed down' stack height is preferable; meaning that the stem is positioned directly on the top race of the headset.

The next time you catch yourself staring at your reflection in a Flemish Mirror or asking one of your riding mates if your back is flat, think of Roger DeVlaeminck. You don't get the moniker Mr Paris–Roubaix by chatting people up down at the corner shop; you get it by winning the Queen of The Classics four times. He was not only a Belgian badass with super-suave sideburns, he was also the epitome of the V-Locus. His position didn't come from £250 bike fits, body-geometry video analysis or ergo-fit shims. It came from a slammed stem and riding his bike. End of.

RULE #46 //
KEEP YOUR BARS LEVEL

Handlebars will be mounted parallel to the ground or angled slightly upward. While they may never be pointed down at all, they may be angled up slightly; allowed handlebar tilt is to be between 180 and 175 degrees with respect to the level road. The brake levers will preferably be mounted such that the end of the brake lever is even with the bottom of the bar. Modern bars, however, dictate that this may not always be possible, so tolerances are permitted within reason. Brake hoods should not approach anything near 45 degrees, as some riders with poor taste have been insisting on doing.

Yes, another basic Rule about bike position, because there are legions of Cyclists with bars turned in all kinds of obscene positions. It gives us all a bad reputation. Bars can rotate completely within the stem clamp and 355 degrees of that rotation are wrong. 'Level' is a difficult term to apply to noodle-shaped tubes.

There are three basic hand positions on the bars: on the tops, behind or on the brake hoods and in the drops. The last two are greatly affected by the handlebar position.

When riding on the tops, the hand transition to the top of the brake levers should be a smooth, slightly downward glide forward. The torso comes down, speed picks up. When in the drops, it's important that the wrists are in a natural angle as one grips the lower bars. Having the right bars at the right angle solves these issues. Ride with an Allen wrench so one can tweak the handlebar angle when first setting up a new bike or a new set of bars. What looks right in the workshop might not be quite right when riding. Even brake lever position can be tweaked after the tape is applied.

If the bike fits the rider, the bars will easily fit the rider and look good on the bike. Click, click, click, the result will be a beautiful unison of human and machine. Both will look good, apart and together.

All lined up and ready for riding.

RULE #50 //
FACIAL HAIR IS TO BE CAREFULLY REGULATED

No full beards, no moustaches. Goatees are permitted only if your name starts with 'Marco' and ends with 'Pantani', or if your head is intentionally or unintentionally bald. One may never shave on the morning of an important race, as it saps your virility, and you need that to kick ass.

Il Pirata climbs so fast, his chin would freeze were it not for the insulative effect produced by this goatee. You are not Il Pirata.

There have really only been two people in the annals of Cycling who have been able to pull off facial hair while still looking badass on the bike; Marco Pantani and the Russian guy in the 1985 movie *American Flyers* (It's worth noting here that only one of these cyclists was real). From a practical point of view, facial hair does not lend itself well to road Cycling. It's too warm, can foul the workings of an otherwise perfect nostril-voiding, and snags in helmet straps. From the viewpoint of the superstitious (which all Cyclists are to some degree) shaving in general needs to be carefully considered as a part of any pre-race ritual. Shave at least a day or two before a race or do what the Italians do so well – show up with five o'clock shadow.

As with many of the Rules, however, all this is really only pertinent to road Cycling in season. Mountain bikers can pretty much rock any type of facial hair their genetics will allow. It is commonly accepted in the cyclo-cross ranks to sport the Dodgy Mo, Soul Patch, or even a full Grizzly Adams. (Of course it also seems acceptable to race cyclo-cross in drag in certain parts of the world, so the acceptability of facial hair should be taken with a grain of whatever grain you find least creditable – salt or otherwise). And if you are caught man-scaping the whiskers on a road bike, it would be best if it were well after Lombardia and sometime before training for next season begins in earnest.

RULE #53 //
KEEP YOUR KIT CLEAN AND NEW

As a courtesy to those around you, your kit should always be freshly laundered and, under no circumstances, should the crackal region of your shorts be worn out or see-through.

Whether riding solo or riding in your dreams while labouring in your awesome cubicle, wear a well kept, clean kit. You are of the Velominati, a shining example to those less enlightened.

This is a given, and requires no discussion. But let's speak to the less enlightened. First, let's speak of the need to ride in a freshly laundered kit. Let us make closer inspection of your 'chamois' after a day's ride (this modern pad, thankfully, is nothing close to a leather chamois as they used to be a score years ago). If ever there were a piece of clothing one would not care to revisit intimately it would be this: sweat, road filth, skin cells, some possible chamois crème frêche, all brewing in the petri dish that is the floor of your bedroom. Is pulling this back on and grinding it all back into your soft tender nether regions for another ride really a good idea? What could go wrong, we ask – besides saddle sores, crotch rot, trench groin, torch-men's taint, and Congo balls? Apaches washed their loincloths in a stream after a full day on the horse. We have no excuse not to. Own a few kits, always ride in a fresh one.

When is a kit too worn? When whoever's on your wheel quickly pulls off, storms by cursing and never lets you move forward in the group. That's when.

RULE #56 //
ESPRESSO OR MACCHIATO ONLY

When wearing Cycling kit and enjoying a pre- or post-ride coffee, it is only appropriate to drink espresso or macchiato. If the word soy/skim latte is heard to be used by a member wearing Cycling apparel, then that person must be ceremonially beaten with CO2 canisters or mini-pumps by others within the community.

What you drink in the privacy of your squalid home is your private matter. What you drink in public, in your nice clean Cycling kit, is not. In Europe, the waiter is allowed to slap your face when you order a soy latté. If he is a good waiter, and you are a Cyclist, he will really step into that slap. Has the world gone mad? Does this have to be spelled out like we are all children here?

Yes, and now that we have Rule #56, the Velominati have no choice. In America, where there are no café waiters to slap some sense into you, the 'barista' (I should be slapped for calling an 18-year-old with eight minutes of training under another 18-year-old a *barista*) already has carpal tunnel syndrome from all the soy-chai-half-decaf lattés they are forced to serve and are no longer able to slap properly.

Think about this. You are pre-ride, in a café waiting in a Casually Deliberate manner for your riding mates. Sitting at a table, resplendent in perfect kit, a delicate espresso cup brought quietly to the lips. Until the ride proves other-wise, you are as cool as the professional at the start village before a mountain stage in the Giro d'Italia.

You are enjoying one of the few legal doping methods enjoyed over the ages. A straight dose of espresso – perhaps a bit of foam to buffer – but really, what would Eddy drink? Seriously, let's call him and ask. OK, we have a restraining order about that but trust us, he does not muck about with soy products.

The caffeine will sharpen the senses, maybe quicken the reaction time when that rabid *blaireau* comes snarling and foaming out of the hedgerow and infiltrates the pace-line. That kid with a stomach full of almond soy milk is the one who goes down and gets a mauling for his mistakes. The caffeine, like all good doping products, provides the rider with a (possibly false) sense of superiority and advantage over their less caffeinated colleagues. You become your own street-legal Ricardo Riccó, taunting your fellow riders for not being as fast as you, whistling as you ride off the front with ease. And like Riccó, it may all come crashing down, so ease off on the taunting and whistling and hope the espresso keeps you riding faster than the aforemen-tioned *blaireau*.

RULE #62 //
YOU SHALL NOT RIDE WITH EARPHONES

Cycling is about getting outside and into the elements and you don't need to be listening to Queen or Slayer in order to experience that. Immerse yourself in the rhythm and pain, not in whatever 80s hair band you call 'music'. See Rule #5 and ride your bike.

Leave the music for the car. You are on your bike and all senses are turned up to 11. Leave the phone calls, leave the music, leave the TwitFace, and leave all your self-involved portal devices in the house. Take the brain and body out for some fresh air. Riding nude might be the most pure way to do it but that always (well, usually) ends badly. A little clothing and a helmet is all that is necessary for the profound experience of riding a bicycle.

Riding any bike, anywhere is good. Riding down Fifth Avenue in New York is amazing, exhilarating. Your skin feels the cool air of the shade then the warmth of the sun as you move down the city blocks. The smells of life are constantly being taken in and processed . . . gaaaggh bus exhaust, eewww something dead, mmmmm doughnuts . . .

Your brain can't be having much more fun than this. The visuals coming in are nearly overwhelming when experienced in motion – no filters, no windscreen glass, just everything streaming in full colour, greyscales, and everything in between. The legs are powered up; keeping up with traffic is the safest and most fun option here, so legs are going at full power. The ears are also picking up the horns, the distant jackhammer, the din of car tyres on asphalt, cars heaving over uneven streets, brakes, motors. It never ends; it's never exactly the same.

Or, when out riding in the high desert, one may only hear the sound of the wind whistling by one's helmet straps and a few bird tweets. Who should deny themselves that lack of noise of civilisation? Why would you?

Our eyes and ears are all we have for sensing the impending metaphorical meteor of doom hurtling in from the beyond. Most often it's what is coming up behind us that is most important and it's the ears that are going to save us from it. A pre-emptive ride into a ditch is not always the worst outcome.

Here are some things you *do* want to hear approaching from behind.

- The kid in cut-offs with the creaky chain – you don't want to hear him as he passes you. You want to hear him from a long way back so you can marshal your forces to keep him back there.
- The rattling scrap metal truck with rusty rebar sticking out the sides of the bed.
- The convoy of trucks hauling oversized, overhanging and unforgiving cement bridge components.
- The station wagon full of drunken teenagers yelling and loading up bottles to throw.
- The rabid badger (see Rule #56).
- The pit bull that just broke its chain. The dog won't be too fast dragging some chain but again, better to start

your sprint with a 30-metre lead than seeing said pit bull snapping at your gleaming calf.

- The ambulance that is clearing traffic onto the shoulder, where you might be.
- A monkey. It's scary enough to be chased by a dog but there are places in the world where a big gleaming black monkey could be closing the distance behind you. Sweet Jesus, that is a nightmare in the making. Why would a monkey do that? Pure mayhem, that's why. It could be brain-infected or just a vengeful beast with horrible teeth and steel springs for arms. I don't know what noises a slightly winded monkey makes as it steadily closes the distance to your rear wheel . . . pat pat pat pat of its feet, at least. If that is drowned out by the Slayer in your earbuds then you, sweet reader, are fucked.

RULE #76 //
HELMETS ARE TO BE HUNG FROM YOUR STEM

When not worn, helmets are to be clipped to the stem and draped over your handlebars thusly.

Fil Potato rolls to the start with a garish but perfectly stored lid.

If your helmet is not on your head, hang it from the stem, forward over the bars, front down. It's secure, symmetrical and looks cool. Here Filippo Pozzato demonstrates Rule #76 as he rides to the start of Milan–Sanremo. Pippo's carefully sculpted hair cannot and will not be crushed under his helmet until the starter's gun goes off.

Feel free to remove your helmet when not riding. Sitting at a café with your helmet on is unnecessary. Your helmet should be hanging off your stem at this point. Granted there is a better than even chance that you will 'take a header' somewhere between your bike and the café table because of your stupid Cycling shoes; a helmet would afford you some cranial protection. Sitting and drinking espresso or beer with your helmet on, it's like wearing your hat in a restaurant. It's not a Rule, just a nod toward civility.

RULE #78 //
REMOVE
UNNECESSARY GEAR

When racing in a criterium of 60 minutes or less the second (unused) water bottle cage must be removed in order to preserve the aesthetic of the racing machine.

A bicycle, by definition, needs two wheels. A strong case can also be made for a frame, chain, pedals, saddle and handlebars. The rest are accessories. No piece of gear is ancillary; each must perform a task and do it well, else it must go.

For a racing bike, this Rule is obvious: every gram counts, so why have extra gear? This approach is just as important to a training bike or commuter, however, because the ride begins with the bike itself. Saddlebags and mirrors are excess not just of the physical, but the metaphysical as well. Strip away the trimmings and the focus of each ride comes quicker, truer and sharper.

What, then, determines necessary? Necessary means not only that the function is needed, but also that the mode is unique – it cannot be achieved by another means. Two wheels? No better solution. A mirror? Well, you could just turn your head. A saddlebag? Your jersey has pockets. A power meter? Just push the pedals harder until either you or the bike breaks.

RULE #80 //
ALWAYS BE CASUALLY
DELIBERATE

Waiting for others pre-ride or at the start line pre-race, you must be tranquilo, resting on your top tube. This may be extended to any time one is aboard the bike, but not riding it, such as at traffic lights.

We, as humans with base level vanity built-in, strive for individuality, a style we can call our own and use as a marker or identifier to stand out from the crowd. Our downfall is that we all seem to draw from the same influences and end up mostly looking like everyone else. The fashion trends of the time dictate to us that the clothes we wear are either *in* or *out*. Being a Cyclist doesn't make it any easier. In fact, it's even harder for a Cyclist to have an individual style when the choices in attire and machine are limited and dictated by the manufacturers. So while choosing your kit carefully helps to cultivate a sense of style, the best way to project an image of calm insouciance is to practise the ancient art of Casj Del.

Casj Del goes back to the times of the early bike racers, with their woollen shorts and 'jerseys', probably handmade by some old Belgian woman with calluses on her fingers to match those on the rider's asses. They looked more like street clothes than riding attire, their eyewear more like welding goggles, their shoes leather and laced. But it was the style these men showed when not riding that stood out even more. Their dark, thick manes of hair precisely cut and slicked back with a thick application of greasy hair pomade. The carrying of a comb was as imperative as carrying a spare tubular wrapped round the shoulders. While they waited for a race to start, or for the prizes to be awarded post-race, they would loiter ever so gracefully among the throngs of excited tifosi, seemingly oblivious to the chaos around them. They would lean against the top tubes of their steeds, maybe poking their nose in the local newspaper, but always with a nonchalant air of comfortable disinterest in their own selves.

They could make sitting on the ground in wet weather look like a desirable pastime, their thin, slick, oily legs positioned at just the right angle to give off an impression of comfort, no matter how uncomfortable they actually were. And when they were on their machines, the smooth and magnificent strokes they emitted as they turned the one and only gear ratio they had – whether up or down an Alp or flying across a valley road – were always the same beautiful cadence that spoke of a lifetime spent honing their craft.

We, as modern-day Velominati, can only aspire to such heights of Casj.Del. Our opportunities are fewer than those of our forebears. We are not superstars and have no tifosi with whom to surround ourselves. Our stage is the roads of our locale; the best we can do is to make our cycling pursuit look as if it is an extension of ourselves.

The bike is our appendage. Our kit is clean, matching and understatedly stylish. We control our breathing, even after ridiculously hard efforts to scale a climb or win a town-line sprint. And we exude this to the various non-cyclists we encounter on every ride, at every set of traffic lights, at every café we may frequent. This is what we do; it's as natural as breathing, maybe even more so. We are casual, and deliberately so.

RULE #82 //
CLOSE THE GAP

Whilst riding in cold and/or Rule #9 conditions replete with arm-warmers, under no circumstances is there to be any exposed skin between the hems of your kit and the hems of your arm. If this occurs, you either need to wear a kit that fits you properly or increase the size of your guns. Arm-warmers may, however, be shoved to the wrists in Five and Dime scenarios, particularly those involving Rule #9 conditions. The No-Gap Principle also applies to knee- and leg-warmers with the variation that these are under no circumstances to be scrunched down round the ankles; Merckx have mercy on whomever is caught in such a sorry, sorry state. It is important to note that while one can wear arm-warmers without wearing knee- or leg-warmers, one cannot wear knee- or leg-warmers without wearing arm-warmers (or a long-sleeved jersey). It is completely inappropriate to have uncovered arms while covering the knees, with the exception of brief periods of time when the arm-warmers may be shoved to the wrists while going uphill in a Five and Dime situation. If the weather changes and one must remove a layer, the knee/leg coverings must go before the arm coverings. If that means that said rider must take off his knee- or leg-warmers while racing, then this is a skill he must master. The single exception would be before an event in which someone plans on wearing neither arm- nor leg-warmers while racing, but would like to keep the legs warm before the event starts; though wearing a long-sleeved jersey over the racing kit at this time is also advised. One must not forget to remove said leg-warmers.

Start in Milan, finish in Sanremo. Fabian Cancellara shows no gaps.

If you wear your jeans hanging halfway down your butt, revealing the brand of your underpants and much, much more than anyone wants or needs to see, or walk around town with your fly undone, your shoelaces untied and your shirt fully unbuttoned to reveal your girlfriends misspelt name tattooed across a fat, hairy gut, then stop reading now. I don't even know why you are here.

For the sane among us, read this Rule again. And once more. Now, refresh your memory with a final pass. Got it? Check your arm-warmers. There, pretty simple, this one. And while you're at it, please make sure that we can't see through the thin material of your worn-out bibs or your tramp stamp poking out where there should be jersey. That could, and should, end in a beating. Seriously.

RULE #95 //
NEVER LIFT YOUR BIKE OVER YOUR HEAD

Under no circumstances is it acceptable to raise your machine above your head. The only exception is when placing it onto a car's roof-rack.

Cyclists aren't weight lifters. Bicycles are not barbells. So why is it that increasing numbers of riders and racers feel the need to lift their bike above their heads, like some sort of trophy or prize, after completing a race or a ride of any magnitude? It doesn't look cool, it proves nothing, and there is nothing to be gained in any performance area.

The arms of a Cyclist are only intended to do one thing: hold the weak upper body up over the front of the bike while the real stars of the show, the legs, do all the necessary heroics. That's why the Cyclist's legs are referred to as "guns," not the arms. Steroid munching meatheads covered in orange paint are the only ones qualified to lift anything above their heads. And this is only because they lack the motor skills and cardiovascular capacity to ride a bike.

This festering blight on the Cycling landscape seemed to start with cross-country mountain bikers, who often finish their race alone and have the time to stop at the line, look around to see if there's actually any spectators in attendance, then bend over like a shaved praying mantis to struggle with the 7 kilogram heft of their carbon hardtail, holding it aloft for the mandatory three seconds until their imaginary judges give the green light to drop it back to earth, its flimsy wheels protesting at the biggest impact they have received after an hour of riding around on groomed tracks devoid of any obstacles that could actually qualify it as mountain biking. Marathon racers are the worst culprits, apparently showing that even after a mind-numbing twenty-four hours of riding in circles, or five days of stage racing through the desert, they still can clean and jerk a quarter of their own body weight.

The recreational Cyclists see these feats of strength and have taken it upon themselves to pose for photographs at the top of iconic road climbs performing their own versions of the Serotta Snatch. Stood in front of famous alpine landscapes or signs telling of the location of their feat, they do nothing except sully these legendary places with this display of pointless posturing. If you see anyone doing this, make them aware that in the eyes of the public who already thinks we look ridiculous in our skintight outfits and shaved legs, that hoisting what amounts to a $7,000 dildo in the air does nothing to further our cause.

Should you be neck deep in a river or for some reason need to throw your bike over a prison wall, exceptions can be made.

PART V:
The Hardmen

Eddy Merckx and Roger de Vlaeminck, two of the hardest men in Cycling and founders of the Eddy and Roger school.

In a sense, the key to becoming a better Cyclist lies in one's capacity to suffer – not only the suffering discipline and dedication of the athlete at work, but also our willingness sacrifice our comfort and warmth in order to submit to our work when the skies are cold and grey and wet with precipitation. We risk crashes and injury; we ride with lumps of our skin missing and bruised joint and limb. The level of physical activity our sport demands of us sends our metabolism skyrocketing, yet we control our appetites in order to shed weight in the hopes of riding ever faster.

Everything about our sport involves suffering, discipline and dedication. In a word, hardness.

A Cyclist is dominated by their will; of knowing we might in some way control our suffering even as we push ourselves harder despite the searing pain in our legs and lungs. Through suffering, we learn something rudimentary about ourselves – that salvation lies at the far side of struggle.

An artist, they say, suffers because he must. A Cyclist, I suggest, suffers because he chooses to. This element of choice, what psychologists refer to as the locus of control, is part of what allows us to feel pleasure through suffering, what allows the pain to be pleasurable. Through this choice unfolds an avenue of personal discovery by which we uncover the very nature of ourselves. Like Michelangelo wielding his hammer to chip away fragments of stone that obscure a great sculpture, we turn our pedals to chip away at our form, eventually revealing our true selves as a manifestation of hard work, determination and dedication to our craft.

Our ability to suffer is driven by our willingness to push ourselves, to resist. Progress equates to the will to resist the signals our bodies are sending. These signals tell us to retire before reaching our mark, to stay inside when the mercury drops or the rain falls. Our will can push us to dip into the cellar for a session on the trainer rather than for a bottle of wine. To walk the path of the Cycling Disciple requires, in considerable quantities, willpower.

Many of the obstacles along that path require us to eschew the wisdom taught to us by society. Listen to your body, you are told, when in fact your body is a chatty thing that has few sensible contributions to make. Stay inside when it's wet, or you'll catch cold, the folk knowledge claims, while in reality those who stay indoors are more likely to catch cold. What doesn't kill you, makes you stronger . . . well, they were bound to get one of them right.

In practice, weakness breeds weakness and strength breeds strength. Taking the easy path is of no use, for nothing worth travelling to lies at its end. We may choose the path of least resistance but this too will ultimately be unsatisfying.

To claim we enjoy suffering, that we enjoy the pain of an effort, or that we enjoy riding in the wet and cold is misleading. While there might be those who possess a perversion that does indeed allow them to actually enjoy pain, for most of us we have merely discovered that the burning of our muscles today strengthens them for tomorrow. We have learned that submitting to the deluge or climbing aboard the trainer in winter helps build towards a result that won't be realised until our planet reaches the next equinox. Rather than enjoying suffering, we enjoy what suffering does for us.

Still, in this sport dominated by suffering, there are some who stand apart in their own realm of hardness. West-Vlaanderen seems to produce the highest concentration (and possibly the largest quantity as well) of this particular breed of Cyclist, collectively known as The Hardmen.

Perhaps it is the weather in that part of the world; perhaps it is the hard-working farming culture that has existed there for centuries; perhaps there is something in the water that makes them crave suffering despite having hosted some of mankind's most vicious battles, but even among Flandrians there is a special breed of rider who is even harder than the Hardmen: the Flahute. The Flahute is the most deranged, and endangered, of all the Cyclists – one who considers the Tour de France little more than good, pleasant-weather training for next year's Spring Classics.

The list of their feats is long. Eddy Merckx stands out as a man for whom beating the competition was secondary to beating himself; when his rivals fell behind, he would attack again just to ensure he suffered sufficiently before reaching the finish line 80 kilometres later and many minutes ahead of the next rider.

The recently deceased Fiorenzo Magni (pictured p.233 in Rule #5) – an Italian with Belgian inclinations – broke his collarbone in Stage 13 of the 1956 Giro d'Italia and used an inner tube clenched between his teeth in order to gain the leverage he needed to continue riding – and finish second.

Johan Museeuw, who nearly lost a leg to a gangrenous knee after crashing in the Forest of Arenberg in the 1998 Paris–Roubaix, fought back to win the race – not once, but twice, in 2000 and 2002.

The list goes on, but suffice it to say that Hardman stands out as a title given to a particularly tough Cyclist – a kind of nobleman of our sport. And as with noblemen, it is a title given, not taken, and begets a set of Rules fundamental to those who strive to reach the upper echelons of The Velominati. Perhaps no other other Rule flows through their blood as deeply or as thickly as the hallowed Rule #5.

RULE #5 //
HARDEN THE
FUCK UP

Any questions?

RULE #9 //

IF YOU ARE OUT RIDING IN BAD WEATHER, IT MEANS YOU ARE A BADASS.PERIOD

Fair-weather riding is a luxury reserved for Sunday afternoons and wide boulevards. Those who ride in foul weather – be it cold, wet, or inordinately hot – are members of a special club of riders who, on the morning of a big ride, pull back the curtain to check the weather and, upon seeing rain falling from the skies, allow a wry smile to spread across their face. This is a rider who loves the work.

Nothing epic ever happens on a sunny day. The legendary battles of Earth's Great Wars were all fought in rain, sleet or snow. The treks of the greatest explorers were undertaken in horrific conditions. When humans finally set foot on another planet, you can bet the weather will suck.

That's the way I like my Cycling, too: rainy, wet, bitterly cold, nasty. Toss in a cobblestone or a cyclo-cross course, and I'm yours for the taking. Kitting up for a rainy ride makes the hairs on the back of my neck stand up in nervous excitement. Pulling my knee- and arm-warmers on and rooting through the bin for a pair of overshoes and long-fingered gloves, I anticipate the cold, wet rain seeping into my pores as it cascades down from above. I know I'll soon be spending my time with thick drops of rain falling from the brim of my cap, acting as my metronome as I carve a solitary trough across the rain-slicked road.

Everything is harder in the rain. Staying warm, for certain. Staying on the bike as well; the rain coaxes all the bits of sand and oil from the tarmac and beckons them to the surface, ready to sweep our tyres out from underneath us. Our stopping distance is stretched, forcing us to be extra-vigilant of hazards; a moment's inattention could be our undoing. Cornering stops being an act of Cycling; it blends instead all the most unsavoury aspects of ice-skating, tight-rope walking, gymnastics and baccarat.

This extra strain keeps us focussed, sharp. Our minds are flushed clean – ancillary thought has no place when riding in such conditions. Contemplation of the cold, the wet or the pain in our legs is dispatched by the total commitment to the craft.

My father taught me at a young age that if I found some-thing unpleasant must be done, there was little sense in not enjoying it. He shrewdly drove this point home by repeatedly having me do things that I didn't enjoy doing. If he noticed I was especially miserable, he would join me in the task and show me that however unpleasant it might be, pleasure can be found in simple things like the acknowl-edgement of progress, appreciating that at some point you'll be done or taking simple satisfaction from the fact that you're pushing yourself to do something you don't want to do. That, in itself, is something to be proud of.

He had a point; you could suffer and hate it or suffer and enjoy it. Fixating on the unavoidable does little to make one feel better about the matter.

Training was a principal tool to demonstrate this lesson. Growing up in Minnesota, there were approximately seven days of pleasant weather each year, and those tended to occur when we were out of state or busy doing something that wasn't training.

That left three hundred and some odd active training days that occurred in unpleasant weather, be it hot, humid, windy, rainy, snowy, frigid, or – on especially unpleasant occasions – an otherworldly combination of all of the above.

Over time, training in bad weather stopped being something I considered a necessity to reach my goals. Instead, knowing that my rivals were sure to be sitting inside waiting for better climes while I was outside being thrashed by the elements became a source of intense motivation. Plus, all of Europe's most notorious races occurred in atrocious downpours, from the Spring Classics, to the Giro and Tour de France, to the World Championships and Fall Classics. Thus, rain quickly became my favourite riding weather.

When I look out the window to see dark skies and sodden roads, a mischievous smile spreads across my face as I realise I'll be able to dress in my Flandrian Best and hurry to kit up and get out before the worst of the weather passes. Few things motivate me more than riding head low into the rain, the brim of my cotton cap shielding my face from the wet and wind, seeing my legs pistoning away clad in knee-warmers, or the feeling of my unzipped gilet flapping in a cold breeze. I imagine myself flying down the narrow tracks of the Flemish countryside in a solo breakaway – which will only just survive to the finish – before crossing the imaginary line in triumph.

Riding in bad weather means you choose the bicycle over

the comfort of the indoors. Riding in bad weather means you prefer engagement and intention to the safety of not taking a risk. Riding in bad weather means you are a badass, period.

RULE #10 //
IT NEVER GETS EASIER,
YOU JUST GO
FASTER

As this famous line by Greg LeMan tells us, training, climbing and racing are hard. They stay hard. To put it another way, per Greg Henderson: 'Training is like fighting with a gorilla. You don't stop when you're tired. You stop when the gorilla is tired.'

Rule #5 plus Rule #5 equals Rule #10. This Rule is deemed so important, it's printed on the Veterminati V-Kit, right there on the right leg, so the rider can read it whilst suffering. It's printed along with Rule #1 and Rule #5: three Rules to ride by.

Greg LeMond originally said it and it speaks to his implausible beginnings. His career was built on a natural talent the rest of us will never experience. LeMond then applied years of hard racing against the greatest of riders like Laurent Fignon, Bernard Hinault and Sean Kelly. Greg was beaten by all of them but handed each of them return beatings that must haunt them when the 2 a.m. Ghosts of Lost Opportunities come calling.

The teenage LeMond was a skier looking for off-season

training. Skiers make good Cyclists: they are usually good descenders; knowing the right line to take through a corner at speed is a skill they already have. Skiers understand that trusting your balance, strength and line gets you through a corner fast. Skiers don't have brakes to engage and it carries over into Cycling. Staying off your brakes is safer and faster but a very hard skill to learn.

As a junior he was beating the seniors, as a senior he was beating the scant few American pros and as a professional he became the youngest World Road Race Champion at age 22. A blue-eyed blond American with the name LeMond winning that race, that young; it came right out of some yet-unwritten fairy tale.

Pure talent got Greg into the European scene but racing at that level is a wicked cocktail of talent, suffering and tactics. Strong riders like Hinault and Kelly were not going to cede any road to the young American, and they knew how to suffer better than anyone in the peloton. Kelly won his early races as a sprinter, Hinault just won his in whatever style it took, tearing off whomever's legs needed to be torn off to win.

Sean Kelly, one of the last of the true Hardmen (who actually hailed from Ireland), was five years older and almost as unlikely to become a Cycling legend as LeMond. He was Sean from County Waterford where Greg was from Reno, Nevada. Both were, inarguably, the greatest cyclists their countries have ever produced. The best riders float to the top in their own countries then migrate to Europe to face off against la crème de la crème.

LeMond and Kelly, then, epitomise Rule #10. But does it apply to us the rest of us? Oh hell yes, it applies to any

Disciple who wants to become a better cyclist. You must venture into the pain cave now and again and if you drop the flashlight in there, even better. Put yourself in situations where the only things that will get you home are heaping helpings of stem, handlebars and riding out of your skin. Don't always save yourself, mess with your riding buddies' minds. Get to the front and tempo it way up for a long time. If you blow and have to limp home, perfect. Do this knowing that the next time you do it, it is bound to hurt as much, only you'll cover more ground in the same amount of time.

RULE #52 //
DRINK IN
MODERATION

Bidons are to be small in size. 500ml maximum: no extra-large vessels are to be seen on one's machine. Two cages can be mounted, but only one bidon on rides under two hours is to be employed. Said solo bidon must be placed in the down-tube cage only. You may only ride with a bidon in the rear cage if you have a front bidon, or just handed your front bidon to a fan at the roadside and are too busy crushing everyone to move it forward until you take your next drink. Bidons should match each other and preferably your bike and/or kit. The obvious exception is the classic Coca-Cola bidon, which by default matches any bike and/or kit due to its heritage. Coca-Cola should only be consumed flat and near the end of a long ride or all-day solo breakaway on the roads of France. Drink in moderation.

We love drinking. Beer mainly, but while our alcoholic tendencies sometimes implore us to fill our bidons with an IPA or a Malteni, common sense rears its ugly, uninvited head and the threat of dehydration looks us dead in the eye, forcing us to the nearest tap. Water is life, life enables us to ride and riding in turn justifies the imbibing of Malted Recovery Beverages after the final shots have been fired from our guns and the last drops of the Essence of V have been wrung from our being.

We are not camels, so carrying more water than we can consume in the time it takes to ride between available refilling stations is unnecessary. Even on the longest of rides on the remotest of roads, there will be ample opportunity to top up bidons from roadside faucets; a service station, a public toilet block, or even the front yard of a residence. There have been times when, in the oppressive heat of an Australian summer, we were able to request refills from kind folk out watering their geraniums or washing the Commodore; several times we received the added comfort of a bidon filled with ice and even electrolyte drink. OK, this may not occur on every ride, but there is always somewhere to get water.

It should go without saying that your bidons match each other, and your bike. Try to avoid team-issue bidons, unless riding a classic team-issue bike. The Coca-Cola bottle is the exception to any non-matching issues, as it has been seen on all manner of team bikes in all the biggest races for many years. It's like a Molteni wool jersey; an icon that has stood the test of time and earned its rightful place in Cycling folklore.

The point is, you do not need to carry oversized, ugly bidons on your bike. What do they offer anyway, an extra 200ml? Hardy enough to mean the difference between dehydration and making it to the next fill point. Actually, that's not really the point either; you know what it's about, and that is making your bike ugly. The same principle that applies to the EPMS, the GPS or mismatched tyres and tape. Small bidons look better, they carry enough liquid and that's all that matters. Plus the less water you drink, the more room is left for Malted Post-Ride Recovery Beverages. You know it makes sense.

RULE #70 //
THE PURPOSE OF COMPETING
IS TO WIN

End of. Any reference to not achieving this should be referred immediately to Rule #5.

We live in a win-at-all-costs society. Even if someone is doing something to the best of their ability, if still they come up short, they are referred to as a loser. Second just isn't good enough any more. Third barely even warrants a look-in.

Except if you're competing against yourself. Or on a particularly challenging course. Or you're riding for your mates. Then we can still achieve a victory, even if the result sheet says we've finished mid-pack. You can lay yourself on the line, literally, and when you're done dishing out The V, the guns with no more ammo left to fire, then you've become a winner.

Of course, this doesn't apply to *actual* racing, where if you aren't the first across the line then there may be more than personal glory at stake. The domestiques, the lead-out men and the climbing lieutenants all share in the spoils if their leader gets to raise his arms, and bear the brunt of blame should they come up short. They will know emotional and physical peaks and troughs on the bike that we mortals could never imagine.

But there is something else to competing. Competing isn't always about planning, it isn't just about calculation. Competing is about *panache*. It's about making a bold move – being willing to risk losing for the chance to win. Certainly, the purpose of competing is to win, but there is a dignity in throwing everything you have at a race and still losing.

This is part of what makes Cycling such a beautiful sport. The lone breakaway, swept up in the final kilometre; the rider who continues on to the finish despite being outside the time limit. The rider whose lead is safe, yet attacks for the glory of attacking and risks losing that precious lead via an unscheduled meeting with the Man with the Hammer.

The purpose of competing is to win, but sometimes the manner in which one loses can outshine the victory.

RULE #71 //
TRAIN PROPERLY

Know how to train properly and stick to your training plan. Ignore other Cyclists with whom you are not intentionally riding. The time for being competitive is not during your training rides, but during competition.

Ask enough old Veliminati what the key to winning races is and soon enough, if not immediately, the answer will be to train properly. Many a wise Cycling Sensei has offered the advice: 'Not going slow enough when you can means you won't go fast enough when you need to.' Indeed, we must train ourselves to go full gas by going full gas – but to a limit. Paradoxically, we must also train ourselves to go fast by taking it easy and sticking to a plan.

We only have so much Rule #5 in The V-Bank available for withdrawal at any given time, so unless your name starts with Eddy and ends with Merckx, you have a finite amount of pain to dish out. The neophyte is marked by taking off up the road every time they make it to the front of the pace-line. The experienced rider is careful not to waste too much energy on rides when goals are being worked towards and the current training ride is simply a means to that end.

One of the keys to training properly is simply to build base kilometres at a slow, easy pace. Pros are fit and fast for many reasons. Their *soigneurs* and team chefs feed them carefully metered calories that are proportioned against the ones burned during the effort of the day. Their bodies are tested like rats in a lab and rockets in wind tunnels for anaerobic and aerodynamic harmony. They ride tens of thousands of kilometres a year, mostly at training pace. And they don't drink much beer, by the way. (Up until that last bit, being a Pro sounded pretty good, didn't it?)

A Velominatus, comparatively, does not have access to personal chefs and wind tunnels and enjoys Malted Post-Ride Recovery Beverages in copious amounts. What we do have access to is kilometres. This, undeniably, is the single best method for building speed, endurance and fitness. Simply ride, as much as you can, at a moderate pace and you will get better. There is a time for riding hard and laying The V down in thick layers, but that time is not when building base kilometres.

Losing this perspective is easy, though, when you see that lone rider 500m up the road and want to grab his wheel and overtake him. Giving it the berries is also tempting when your riding mates are spurring you on, especially when you know you're on form and really want to show those fat tits the damage your guns can exact. What's more difficult is staying off the rivet when your legs are telling you to kill it on Thursday but your mind is telling you to save it for Saturday's criterium. The Cycling Disciple must trust in the plan they developed to meet their goals. Holding back when we should allows us to dig deeper when we need to.

Rule #71 offers the Velominatus many lessons in one simple Rule. Primarily it is that there is more to winning bike races than speed alone. One must learn to quiet one's mind when it is screaming to jump after the rider who launches the go-nowhere breakaway in the false hope of garnering meaningless bragging rights at the après-velo café. Rule #71 tells us to be patient, to trust in our preparations. It tells us that commitment wins over raw strength almost every single time.

RULE #72 //
LEGS SPEAK
LOUDER THAN WORDS

Unless you routinely demonstrate your riding superiority and the smoothness of your Stroke, refrain from discussing your power meter, heart rate or any other riding data. Also see Rule #74.

Let your legs do the talking. No one cares what your power-to-weight ratio is, unless that ratio is V. No one cares about your weekly miles or your Strava KOM status on some obscure 'climb'. This is all valuable information, but only to you. So keep it that way. Bragging about your cycling stats is the equivalent of the 'I've just made an AWESOME sandwich! Mmm – oniony!' Facebook status.

Let your legs tell everyone a little story about your magnificent stroke, your souplesse of cadence and your easy pedalling efficiency on a climb. If you need to speak, speak of the great Italian Cyclist Gianni Bugno as you climb in a group. Regale them with stories of the stillness of his upper body as he mashed a monstrous bear of a gear up the *cols* of the Tour de France,. Of his using his sprint to win back-to-back World Championships, of his 1990 Giro d'Italia victory where he wore the *Maglia Rosa* from the first stage to the last. Tell them how he defeated Belgium's own Johan Museeuw in the Ronde van Vlaanderen and how Gianni took the Lion's dinner right off his plate in front of his own countrymen. Then you ask the question.

'He was a strong man, no?'

If your legs have really been doing more talking than you, everyone will be struggling to breathe, let alone talk. Their best verbal response might be a huffed, 'Yeah'. Otherwise a grunt or a nod will indicate to both you and them that your legs have spoken louder than your stories. As the going gets tough, talking is the first thing to stop. The conversation your legs can lead is always more impressive than what's coming out of your mouth.

RULE #90 //
NEVER GET OUT OF THE BIG RING

If it gets steeper, just push harder on the pedals. When pressed on the matter, the Apostle Johan Museeuw simply replied, 'Yes, why would you slow down?' It is, of course, acceptable to momentarily shift into the inner ring when scaling the 20% ramps of the Kapelmuur.

Pavé Cycling Classics–Velominati's Keepers Tour: Cobbled Classics 2012 was, for most of us, our first time on the cobbles of Northern France and Belgium and certainly our first time meeting the last Lion of Flanders. The first thing I noticed about Johan Museeuw was his ass. It's not that I was looking for it, it's just that it happened to be the first thing I was presented with.

We were supposed to be back at the gîte by noon, but none of us could get our act together quite quickly enough to be there on time. We arrived a bit late and we huddled outside to organise ourselves and to work out a strategy on how we could best preserve our composure upon meeting one of the greatest living legends of our sport.

Our strategy hadn't accounted for the possibility that Johan Museeuw would be butt-naked when we arrived. We'd forgotten to take into account that this was Europe, where people have a tendency to be naked at surprising times.

There he was, at the top of the stairs, baring his magnificent ass to our group. Right. We're kitting up then, I presume.

Rolling out with Museeuw was a surreal experience. He wasn't as thin as he was when he was racing and he wasn't wearing his Mapei or Quickstep kit. He also wasn't wearing his Briko sunglasses or his trademark hairnet and Cycling cap. But he *was* still Johan Museeuw; his position on the bike, the look in his eyes and the action of his pedal stroke were all unmistakeable. On several occasions I felt as though I was watching an old race video. Only now it was in 3D Hi-Def Blu-ray Surround Sound with Surround Smell (3DHDBRSSSS).

Off we headed through the farmlands around Kemmel, through the heart of where World War I was fought. The roads upon which we rode were also the site, much more recently, of the Gent–Wevelgem semi-classic. As we began a gentle climb, Johan pointed to the right and said, 'Turn right, the race used to take us up this way.'

Since none of us were in a mood to argue with a Legend, we all turned and headed up in the direction he had instructed. I happened to be riding next to him, and the road steepened quickly – as they tend to do in this part of Belgium. I grabbed a handful of front shifter and dropped into the little ring in order to accommodate the rude gradient.

Next to me, Museeuw just kept pedalling. Nothing about him changed. It was as if the road were still level.

As the road narrowed, we came to ride closer together, the way we Cyclists are wont to do. As the road also began to twist, we occasionally brushed shoulders as we went round bends. The road steepened ever more and the twists turned into switchbacks.

As is typical of such roads, the hairpin bends were steepest on the inside, and as we went around a left-hander Museeuw found himself smack on the inside with no choice but to ride through the steepest bit. Off on the outside, it was much less steep, but, even there, I found myself reaching for another gear with which to ease the pressure in my legs.

And next to me, Museeuw just kept pedalling. Nothing about him changed. It was as if the road were still level.

We reached the top of the climb with Museeuw holding a small lead over me, and as the road actually did level back out, I clawed my way back alongside him.

'Oh, I see how you do that. When the road gets steep, you don't slow down. You just keep going the same speed as before.' I spoke to him in his native Flemish, hoping my Dutch accent and huffed words wouldn't mask my sarcasm.

He looked at me for a long moment; I couldn't see his eyes behind his sunglasses, but I could tell he was not quite sure what I was asking, and wasn't sure that I wasn't taking the piss.

Finally, he responded. 'Yes, Why would you slow down?'

RULE #91 //
NO FOOD
ON TRAINING RIDES UNDER
FOUR HOURS

This one also comes from the Apostle Johan Museeuw, who said to Frank: 'Yes, no food on rides under four hours. You need to lose some weight.' Or, as Fignon put it, sometimes, when we train, we simply have to go out to meet the Man with the Hammer. The exception is, of course, hard rides and races of more than an hour. Also, if you're planning on being out for more than four hours, start eating before you get hungry. This also applies to energy-drink supplements.

As Eddy Merckx is The Prophet, so the Man with the Hammer is Saint Veter, standing at the Great Cog, choosing who is to be allowed into the realm of the Velominati.

My induction into this particular world started at a young age. As many families do, we took our bikes with us on family vacations. The only difference was that we normally left the car at home.

These Cycling vacations were unsupported by SAG wagons or any such convenience; we rode through communities and cities as we made our way along our route. We carried food and supplies as any reasonable person would, but should one of us have an unscheduled visit with the Man with the Hammer, there was simply no alternative but to continue riding until we reached the next town, which was usually more than a few kilometres too far away.

By the time I was eight or nine years old, I had already met the Man with the Hammer more times than anyone outside my nuclear family. I quickly came to know him only too well, such that I started expecting him at family gatherings like weddings, birthday parties, Christmas and other family gatherings.

Of these many meetings, there are two occasions that stand out as the most monumental. The first occurred in the spring of my seventeenth year, the second in the winter of my thirty-fifth.

When I was 17, my dad took me to Belgium to ride the cyclosportif of Liège–Bastogne–Liège. It was April or May, and I was in the form of my life; over the winter, I had become State Champion in Nordic ski racing, and the momentum had carried into an early spring season of training on the bike. Not only that, but I had also managed to scrape the cash together for a Selle San Marco Regal saddle and a pair of Scott Drop-In handlebars; with my bike set up just like Greg LeMond's, I was sure to be unstoppable.

Being Dutch, we flew in to Amsterdam, stayed a day or two with family who no doubt assumed we were insane (and were quite likely right) and set out by bicycle for the start of the ride in Liège, some 400km away.

We had a cosy two days to get there, so I am at a loss to remember precisely why that seemed like such a long distance, but it did.

We didn't call ahead for hotels, instead making it up as we went along; one hotel somewhere near the Dutch border in Belgium and another in Liège. We rode our race bikes with the most enormous European Posterior Man-Satchels you've ever seen. They were made by Blackburn and held everything we needed for the entire five-day trip. They weighed as much as tanks and swayed about under our saddles like a prize bull's scrotum.

As it turned out, the most brilliant tactical manoeuvre we made was not to book the hotel in Liège for two nights; we made it for one and took our prosthetic bull scrotums with us on this, the most hilly of the Spring Classics. Ironically, that decision took balls.

The first half of the ride was fine; the route from Liège to Bastogne is not particularly difficult. It was fine, indeed, but for one minor detail. White arrows marked this year's route while the year previous had used blue arrows. It was a clever idea to use two different-coloured arrows to distinguish between years. What the organisers had neglected to realise, however, was that blue looks an awful lot like white after sitting out in the elements for a year.

I can't be sure if anyone else made the same error, but we didn't catch on until we had enjoyed a lovely, sweeping descent of 50 kilometres into a picturesque village with a bridge that crossed over a majestic river. Even now, I can see it before me as though I were there. And I can still see Steven Roche's name on that bridge, in giant white block letters.

The only problem was that Steven Roche had retired the year before. We were on the previous year's route.

Since Google Maps was Science Fiction and mobile phones hadn't made it off the set of *Miami Vice*, we had no alternative but to turn our bikes on their back wheels and head back up what was now a sweeping, 50 kilometre climb back out onto the ridge whence we had come.

After working out the arithmetic on Liège–Bastogne–Liège, which is a ride of around 260 kilometres, by the time we reached the turnaround point in Bastogne, which represents the approximate midway point of the race, we had covered something like 230 kilometres.

We were approaching the famous Côte de la Haute-Levée, which appears at around 180km in the route, or 280km for us, given our detour. I was on my dad's wheel, riding along like I had for much of the day when suddenly the gap between his back and my front tyres began to open up.

I pushed harder on the pedals and nothing happened. Then I pushed a bit harder still. Nothing. Before long, I saw him look under his arm and note with some surprise that I was no longer behind him. He sat up. He waited. I didn't feel like I was getting closer.

The details from this particular period of time get hazy, as they tend to do when getting walloped by The Man with the Hammer, but I remember two things in particular. One is lying under a big tree and a woman feeding me round tablets that I think were supposed to go in a bidon of water to make energy drink. They went down pretty easy in solid form, if I recall correctly.

The second thing I remember is us stopping at a café on a descent just before the Haute-Levée and my dad ordering basket after basket of frîtes served up the only way the

Flandrians know how to serve them, with a giant glob of mayonnaise. He maintains that we were six baskets in before the colour came back into my cheeks.

I wasn't keeping count, as I was preoccupied by the sight of the Haute-Levée just outside of town; it looked impossibly steep from where we were sitting, and I could see the other riders doing the paperboy up the steep grade. I didn't stop eating until I thought I could make it up the hill with that infernal saddle pack dragging me back down.

When we finished the route, we had an enormous dinner and set about finding another hotel where we could stay the night. We wound up at the same hotel, in the same room. To add 100 kilometres onto the toughest Ardennes classic route was bad. To do that route needlessly carrying shampoo, clean underwear and five days' worth of unessential essentials was cause to call Child Services. Was the Old Man passing on his knowledge of Rule #5 the only way he knew how? Or was he simply not quite as clever and a bit more Dutch than my 17-year-old self had made him out to be? It didn't really matter. I had met the Man with the Hammer again and rode away stronger for it.

Until last year, that was the only time I had my goose cooked completely by the Man with the Hammer. But in my training for Velominati's annual pilgrimage to the Spring Classics in the Keepers Tour, I indulged in 200-kilometre solo training rides in the hills surrounding Seattle. These hills are not dissimilar to the *cotes* of Belgium: a few kilometres in length and usually numbering more than one but seldom more than three. On a route totalling 200 kilometres, it is not uncommon to cover two or three kilometres in vertical elevation gain.

Winters in Seattle are characterised by rain and the mercury's tendency to hover tauntingly around the freezing level. Aside from Belgium, the Pacific Northwest of the United States is about as Rule #9 as it gets anyplace else on earth. Training there in the winter for the Classics in the spring is a good proving ground.

I live in a part of Seattle called Phinney Ridge that, not surprisingly, sits atop a not insignificant ridge. I set out at 7 a.m., when the sun had just crept high enough above the trees to illuminate the streets, and felt optimistic about the possibility of staying dry that day. However, the clouds grew ever darker until they finally relinquished their grip on the rain they held and let it plummet to the ground.

The temperature dropped, the rain fell and on I rode, alone. I headed into the mountains and their higher ground where I would ride out the second half of my route. The temperature continued to fall and I found myself reaching for food more often in an effort to stay warm, given the extra energy I was expending in the cold and wet.

As I topped Cougar Mountain, some 70km from home, I was riding in the snow, without food and in dimming light.

When I was a kid, there was a comic strip in the newspaper about a sergeant in the army who was plagued by a lazy corporal. The strip was made bearable by another corporal who was an idiot. I remember one particular strip that featured the idiot driving a jeep back to camp like they were being chased by the devil himself. The sergeant, who was in the passenger seat, queried the idiot as to why he was driving so fast. The idiot replied that the jeep was low on fuel and he wanted to get to base before it ran out of gas.

I rode home like that idiot drove his jeep.

I almost made it, but not quite. As I entered town, I found myself slowing for traffic lights before they turned yellow; I was eager for the excellent excuse to stop and rest. After a few of these lights, I found myself resting my head on the handlebars as I waited for the lights to turn green again. After a few more lights, I found myself waking up when the motors in the cars alongside me roared to life when the light changed.

When I eventually got to the base of Phinney Ridge – a mere 50 metres from my home – I got off my bike and sat at the roadside, trying to figure out how I was going to get up the hill. I wound up riding up it, and I remember it wasn't as bad as I imagined it would be, but I can't really be more specific than that. We have already established that no one is walking up anything in this Cycling life. When the tank has nothing in it but stale vapours and the guns of Navarone are overheated, warped and useless from relentless six-hour shellings, we go back to the fundamental Rule: Rule #5. We go back to the basics of simply turning the pedals. You don't have to figure out how you're going to ride all the way home; you just have to figure out how you're going to turn the pedals one more time.

Finale

Every great race features a great ending, the Finale. The Champs Elysees, the Roubaix Velodrome, The Poggio and the Muur de Huy are as iconic as the races in which they feature. Sometimes the race has been decided long before it reaches the line, other times it comes down to the last metres. Whether it takes six hours or three weeks, the journey to reach the finish is always filled with drama and fraught with challenges that each and every rider must overcome, whether fighting it out for the win or merely to get to the finish before the time limit.

This book has taken us across rough pavé and over high alpine passes, up impossibly steep and narrow climbs. We have ridden together in a grupetto and sprinted headlong down wide boulevards. And, like any race, there were times when we hit the wall but knew if we kept at it we would recover and finish strongly. And just as the races finish and the riders climb off their bikes weary and battered, they know that their work will commence again the next day, and the day after and they will strive to do their job better than the previous time, again and again.

A Velominatus lives by the same ethos, continuing to look for ways to improve our riding, our passion for it, our enjoyment of it. We seek new means to look and feel better about ourselves, our bikes and our etiquette while we ply our craft.

With The Rules currently numbering 91, we know that they will continue to develop, be added to, refined and defined as we ride along the road of La Vie Velominatus. We receive suggestions for new Rules almost daily, and some of them have made it into the tome you have read here. The Rules are not static; they are a living, growing, evolving thing that develops with our sport and one which is brought to life by you. You help to make The Rules; the Keepers merely do our best to curate and maintain them.

The Rules help us find new reasons to ride our bikes every day; our hope is that they help you do the same. None of this matters if we don't find reason to throw our leg over a top tube as often as we can.

Thank you for reading, and thank you for being a part of our community.

Vive La Vie Velominatus.

Acknowledgements

If one is to venture into the archives of Velominati, to the oldest articles found therein, you will find short conversations consisting mostly of the five Keepers, and the occasional oddball reader, going back and forth.

A lot has changed for us since those days, but one thing has always been constant; our passion for the bike, and the enjoyment in discussing it with anyone who wishes to participate. We laugh, we tell jokes, we spin wildly off topic, we insult each other, we argue, we make up.

That spirit of openness of sharing and communication has brought Velominati to the point where it is now. Each and every reader and Community member has contributed their part to help make Velominati one of the fastest-grown Cycling communities in the world. We could never have had the opportunity to bore you with this book had it not been for you. From the bottom of our hearts: thank you.

We would like to thank a few members of our community have stood out and been particularly helpful and inspiring.

Michelle, for her love and support to Frank, and for never telling him how stupid his ideas are.

Frank's Family Andrine, Otto, Erik, and Karen, who all helped him discover and cultivate a love for the bike at a young age, riding together on sacred roads all over Europe.

Brett's parents Brian and Christina, who have supported his cycling from an early age with the constant drain of new bikes, new parts, and his dragging mud, grease and blood throughout the house for so many years. You helped him believe he could make his passion his profession.

Gianni's wife Beth, for shaming him into more riding than he sometimes wants to do and to Mark Lowrey for steering him into this glorious Cycling Life.

Marko's family, Sheri and Isla, who have encouraged him to live Rule #11 more than any wife and daughter reasonably should.

Jim's saddle, though it is a poor substitute for a bar stool.

Johnny Klink, who co-coined the term 'The Rules' with Brett during those nights in the shed, tinkering with their machines to get them just right. His attention to detail bordering on the obsessive set an example for everyone to follow.

Col, whose bikes and attire inspired the notion that both should always Look Fantastic, because his rarely did. Despite this, he still kicked ass on and off the bike.

James Spackman, for reaching out with a crazy proposal to write a book on The Rules, and for guiding us through the proposal process.

Drummond Moir, for patiently tolerating our collective obsessive-compulsive natures in order to actually write and finish the book.

William Fotheringham, for being an inspiration over the years providing the English-speaking world with our doses of superb Cycing journalism. Also for being a supporter of the community, and kindly writing the forward for our book.

Angelo Giangregorio (AKA Pedale.Forchetta), for being a respected and long-standing member of our community and generously allowing us to use his phenomenal photos in our book.

Jesse Willems (www.jessewillems.be), for being a fan and supporter, and for allowing us to use the photos from Keepers Tour: Cobbled Classics 2012 in our book.

Jeremy Kershaw, for allowing us to use his photo of Marko from the 2012 edition of The Heck of the North.

Levi Lexvold, for learning to write 'Harden the Fuck Up' in a dead Viking language and allowing us to render it on The Prophet's stone tablets.

Picture Acknowledgements

Gianni Andrews: 87. Marko Carlson: 36, 138. Cor Vos/Cor Vos Fotopersburo-Video ENG: 14 (head), 26, 66, 159, 161, 173, 177, 190, 201, 218. Elizabeth Keller: 75. Jeremy Kershaw: 184. Pedale Forcheta: 158, 200, 210, 217. Getty Images: 78/AFP/Pascal Pavani, 100/Roger Viollet, 192/AFP. Ronald Grant Archive: 14 (background). Het Laatste Nieuws: 15. Photosport Int/Rex Features:191. Jean-Yves Ruszniewski/TempSport/Corbis: 180, 102. Frank Strack: 121, 135. Jesse Willems: 42, 88, 105, 170.

The Lexicon

A-MERCKX // **A declaration of affirmation used by a Velominatus.** This can be used in many conversational instances or when in worship as a concluding word for prayers and hymns to the Great Gods of Cycling. (This is not to be confused with the first initial and last name of Eddy Merckx's son, Axel.)

ADRIAN // **Being an annoying, if harmless, twatwaffle.** An Adrian also exhibits poor spelling and grammar while attempting to make points on velominati.com.

THE ANTI-V // **The forces in life that cause you to not observe The V.** The Anti-V manifests itself in an absence of those things we love most about cycling: a combination of guts, class, and panache. Wheel-sucking, bragging, and poor sportsmanship are examples of The Anti-V.

ARISTOCRATS // **White/black cycling shoes.** The combination of white and black in a fine Italian patent leather shoe.

BEL MEZZO // **Mezzo in Italian vernacular stands for means of transport.** I'm showing you my new bike and you say: Bel Mezzo!

BELGIAN STYLE // **Riding primarily with hands positioned on the hoods.** 'Look how clean the tape is on that dude's drops! He must be a Belgian Style specialist.'

BELGIAN TOOTHPASTE // The thick, sticky spit you get when laying down The V.

BELLY BREATHING // Excusing a gut as a breathing technique. The assertion that one is not sporting a protruding gut but is in fact using a highly sophisticated respiration technique called diaphragmatic breathing.

BLACK WIDOWS // Black cycling shoes. Preferably made of patent-leather and by an Italian cobbler.

BREEDING AND BLIMPING // Having kids and gaining weight. The process of gaining weight after becoming a parent due to a shift in priorities.

BRIAN // Brian will crush your ego and is of the same sub-species as Adrian. The guy who bridges up to you on a ride, usually a climb, wearing items like khaki shorts, a camelbak, and clip-ons, breaking any given number of Rules and then proceeds to ride you off his wheel.

BRO-SET // SRAM. Since Gruppo is an Italian word, the only Gruppo is Campagnolo. Shimano is a Group-san, and SRAM is a Bro-Set.

BROMMER // Motorcus's bike. Derived (read: taken wholesale) from the Dutch word for moped.

CADELEPHANTIASIS // A sudden increase in tough-ness and aggressive riding. Specifically, the increasing in size of one's gonads to gargantuan proportions when exposed to rainbows, as was the case with Cadel Evans.

CARBON CRAPLET // The carbon framed bikes that are passed on a climb or sprint. This is best emphasized as you hammer on your Old Skule steel. e.g 'I dropped a half dozen Carbon Craplets on the River Road sprint.'

CARBONE // That feeling you get when you see a beautiful bike.

CASUALLY DELIBERATE // The easy sense of style and calm exuded by a Velominatus. This is true whether they are on the bike, off the bike and is exhibited by a sharp dress sense and air of confidence.

CHARISMATICALLY POISONED // Carrying a good beer buzz. Its a scientifically proven fact that people are more charismatic when drinking alcohol. Alcohol is also a poison. Thus, drinking makes us charismatically poisoned.

CHICKED // Getting your ass dropped by a Velominata. We're all Peaking in Two Months; set your male insecurities aside and train harder, jackhole.

CLIMB WELL FOR MY WEIGHT // Being a good climber relative to your weight/size. The assertion that despite your size, you are still a reasonable climber.

CLIMBONE // That feeling you get when you see a beautiful climb.

COBBLEBONE // That feeling you get when you see an roughly paved road. This is most acutely felt in the presence of rough cobblestones. Paradoxically, upon riding cobbles, the absence of feeling is often the result.

COGAL // A meeting of Velominati for a day of cycling and beer. Just as the Illuminati would stage their fabled, and somewhat feared Cabals, the Velominati stage our own modern-day versions, the Cogals. A meeting of like-minded misfits brought together by the promise of beer, preceded by a bike ride. A Cogal distinguishes itself from other group rides by the following criteria. First, Cogals are organized and supported through Velominati, though not necessarily a Keeper (legally speaking, however, we have no involvement, so if you crash or die, it's your own problem). Second, a Cogal is a day-long undertaking that focuses 100% on the bike. The rides are categorized (Casually Deliberate, Rule #5, Rule #10, for example) but are long. This is what you're doing today, nothing else; see Rule #4. Third, Cogals always include a session of Malted Recovery Beverage Consumption after the ride. Whenever possible, it should also include a pre-ride espresso.

COGNOSCENTI // *The sect of Rule #5 Fundamentalists.* We don't strictly endorse their interpretation, but like the Catholics and Opus Dei, we recognize them as part of our own.

COGNOSCENTRIX // *A female Rule #5 Fundamentalist.*

COGNOSCENTUS // *A Rule #5 Fundamentalist.*

COMMUNING WITH BUTTERFLIES // *Climbing so slowly that butterflies nest in your spokes.* 'The last time I climbed it a butterfly flew through my front wheel completely unscathed.'

COMMUTER GRAND PRIX // *The domain of the Cycleway Hero.* Only they know where the intermediate sprints, KOM and finish line is, and they are never beaten.

COTHO // *C*nt Of The Highest Order.* See also Pharmstrong, Veino, Pharmstrong, Contador, Pharmstrong, Piti, Johan Bruyneel, Pharmstrong, Ricco, Hein Verbrugge, and Pat McQuaid – depending on your perspective.

CYCLEWAY HERO // *Cyclists who treat their daily commute as races.* The commute is seen as a way to prove their manhood by wheel-sucking, or blasting past on their squeaky MTBs whilst wearing a YJA. Never says 'hello'. Considers fellow commuters to be their competition and sworn enemies.

CYCLING SENSEI // *A Velominatus' highly revered mentor.* This mentor teaches and guides us in the finer ways of our Sport.

CYCLING SHIT SANDWICH // *A triathlon.* Also referred to as the CSS, the Cycling Shit Sandwich is characterized by an event which begins with prolonged near-drowning and ends with trying to outrun the slowest person in your vicinity. May also involve a conclusive demonstration of a lack of motor skills.

DARK KNIGHTS // **An alternative moniker for The Black Widows.**

DELGADO // **Missing the start of the VSP or any other event.** Inspired by Pedro Delgado's 1989 late Tour start as defending champion.

DIRTY SCHLECK LOVE // **The illogical hero-worship of any cyclist.** Particularly one who has yet to make the most of his ability. It is the velomotion that daren't speak its name.

DORK DISK // **The useless plastic guard that is installed on bicycles.** This part exists for the same reason as blue M&Ms: one we can't explain.

DOTTY JUMPER // **The Polka-Dot jersey.** The spotted jersey given in the drug-riddled King of the Mountains competition at the Tour de France.

DUTCH GEL SHOT // **A packet of mayonnaise.**

EPMS // **Velomiskrit for European Posterior Man Satchel.**

ESCAPE VELOCITY // **The speed at which you spin out your top gear.** This is the critical point at which all speed has been coaxed from your machine and you have wrung the top end out of your block. 'I hit Escape Velocity on that descent and I had to break out my LeMond tuck.'

EUROPEAN POSTERIOR MAN SATCHEL // **A saddlebag.**

FENDANGELIST // **Fender (mud guard) evangelist.** A rider who insists on pointing out and scolding riders in a group who fail to ride with fenders, pointing out the many reasons they should do so in the future.

FIVE AND DIME // Laying down The V in the whole-sale commitment to Rule #10.

FLANDERS FACIAL // Covering your face in mud and grit while riding. The fashionable 'in' look of the Spring season whereby the cyclist's face is caked with mud in the tradition of the Spring Classics. Note: any mud will do, not just Flandrian mud.

FLANDRIAN BEST // Arm warmers, vests, Belgian booties, and a cap under the helmet. While church goers will dress in their Sunday Best for a sermon, when a Cyclist goes to worship in bad weather, they dress in their Flandrian Best.

FLEMISH TAN LINES // Artificial tan lines caused by mud, grit, and cow shit. After a Rule #9 ride, the contrast between one's clean and grit-covered skin is directly proportional to how awesome the ride was.

FLEMISH MIRROR // The reflection of a rider caught in the shiny, rain-soaked tarmac.

FLUIDLY HARMONIC ARTICULATION // Riding in harmony with the bicycle. This refers to the symbiotic relationship between oneself and one's machine. It is characterised by an immovable torso combined with effortlessly gliding pedal rotations. A revelation of harmony and elegance for you resulting in high doses of Rule #5 pain for your fellow riders. This is a state only obtainable when peaking, and is sometimes referred to as La Volupté.

FUCKNESS // Any manner of negative physiological effects caused by weather.

GLORIOUS STEEL // The exclamation that steel is the finest material for a bicycle. See also, Steel is Real.

GOLDILOCKS PRINCIPLE // Ensuring that bibs and socks are not too long or too short. Also applies to any other matter of Good Taste and Sensibility where extremes are unpalatable.

GRAVEUR // A rider who specializes on riding gravel roads. Whether its the white Tuscan roads of the Strade Biancha, the roughly graded clay backroads of Northern Minnesota, or the stone gravel mountain passes of the Rocky Mountains, the Graveur knows some of the best riding is to be had off the beaten path of tarmac. A Graveur's rig generally resembles a CX bike modified slightly for longer rides at higher speeds, but can also be a road bike with extra-wide and durable tyres.

GROUP-SAN // Shimano. Since Gruppo is an Italian word, the only Gruppo is Campagnolo. Shimano is a Group-san, and SRAM is a Bro-Set.

GRUPPO // Campagnolo. Since Gruppo is an Italian word, the only Gruppo is Campagnolo. Shimano is a Group-san, and SRAM is a Bro-Set.

GUN CHECK // An assessment of the state of your legs. How much hurt your legs have absorbed, and how much hurt they are capable of dishing out at any given moment. Whatever you're doing now, can only be sustained for V more minutes. Own your guns.

GUN DECKS // The platforms that absorb the massive force of our guns. Every Velominatus knows their guns aren't their arms (carry those gallons of milk in one at a time, we don't want to build up too much upper body mass, Hercules) but their legs. And we all know the way to make our bikes go faster is to push harder on the Gun Decks, also known as pedals.

HANDLEBAR DINGLEBERRY // A loose, loopy bit of handlebar tape. See also Hasidic Handlebars.

HARDMAN // The tough-as-nails cyclist. Often spotted gliding over cobblestones or mashing up the Koppenberg in the Big Ring in all kinds of weather. This one is not ours, but it bears inclusion here since we use it so much.

HARDMANIFESTO // **The Fundementalist Manifesto followed by the Cognescenti.**

HUANGISM // **A trite and/or clichéd remark about a bike.** Commonly made by CyclingNews.com technical editor, James Huang, whose reviews are sometimes nothing but cliché-riddled re-hashes of manufacturers' press releases. An example of a Huangism is a statement like 'laterally stiff, vertically compliant'.

INHALING A WASP // **Gasping for air whilst climbing.** Mouth agape, snarling, dishing out the V.

LIKE FUCK YOU WILL // **A partner's level of faith in a Cyclist's follow-through.** A spouse's assertion that any promise made towards post-ride activity will be superseded by laying on the couch, complaining about your guns.

LUGGS // **Lugs so sexy they deserve a second 'g'.**

MACH V // **The speed attained by maximum application of Rule #5.** This requires whole-body commitment to Sur La Plaque; a profound Knowledge of Rule #85 and Rule #64 are especially important.

MAGNIFICENT STROKE // **A rider's smooth, powerful stroke.** *Pedal* stroke.

THE MASTURBATION PRINCIPLE // **Rule violations are like masturbation.** The Keepers understand that from time to time, some riders will violate a Rule or two because of their personal situation. If this is the case, we understand you might do it, but don't fucking brag about it. Also like masturbation, it is best done where no one can see you and too much of it will make you go blind.

MILLARCOPTER // **The arcing, spinning motion of a thrown bike.** This is normally taken on by a bike when ejected over a fence, or the destination of your choice. Of course, we would never treat our bikes like this, because we pay for ours.

MINI-PUMPS AT DAWN // Challenge to a duel. Them's fightin' words! A Velominatus' version of the 'Gentleman's Duel' of the past.

MOUNT VELOMIS // The mountain within whose fiery depths were forged The Rules.

NEARLY PEAKING // Assertion that you are no longer Too Fat To Climb. Also may mean to imply that you are in training and approaching form.

ONYX BLAHNIKS // Black fi'zi:k R1's. This could also apply the white R1's as Onyx technically refers to a spectrum of colors. In any case, these shoes set the standard.

OSCARITO PRINCIPLE // Gaffer-taping a mini-pump to your frame.

OUT OF DISH // When someone is acting out of order. 'Hincapie was really Out of Dish blaming the others in the break for not chasing. What a COTHO!'

PEAKING IN TWO MONTHS // Being out of form and overweight. A universal acknowledgement that one is out of form and overweight, while at the same time asserting that you are following a strict training plan and diet and that when you do peak – in two months – you will dish out pain in overwhelming proportions.

PEDALWAN // A Cycling Sensei's protegé.

PHANTOM AEROBARS // Resting the forearms on the tops of the bars. Getting low and aero on standard road bars as if they were riding on aerobar extensions, á la Fabian Cancellara.

PITI PRINCIPLE // Punishment for violating the spirit of the law. A model of punishment wherein a competitor is sanctioned for abusing the system while still technically staying within the specific guidelines.

POST GT DEPRESSION // **Depression suffered at the conclusion of a Grand Tour.** The onset of a sense of hopelessness characterized by irritable and manic behavior as access to cycling coverage decreases suddenly from daily to weekly (or less). Treatments include Rule #5, riding, and Rule #5.

POST-RIDE RECOVERY ALE // **See Post-Ride Recovery Drink.**

POST-RIDE RECOVERY DRINK // **A nice, cold, hoppy ale.** Consumed after a hard ride to restore carbohydrates, proteins, sugars, and Awesome to the body.

PRE-RACE KELLY // **Going without sex.** Usually involuntarily and often a result of some action involving That Fucking Bike. This can also be a deliberate, voluntary pre-race preparation technique in the spirit of Sean Kelly.

THE PRINCIPLE OF SILENCE // **The notion that your bicycle must always be quiet.**

RAINBOW TURD // **Wearing over-matched rainbow kit.** Wearing full matching white rainbow jersey with white rainbow bibs, and then being crapped out of the back of the bunch when the road goes uphill, as Mario Cipollini did in the 2002 Giro d'Italia.

RECOVERY RIDE SPECIALIST // **A rider who never participates in hard rides.** One who is always on a recovery ride everytime you go out for a spin because they 'hit it so hard the previous day'. Of course, no one is ever with them when they actually do a hard ride. See also Train Properly.

RED DAMSELS // **Red cycling shoes.** Preferably made of patent-leather and by an Italian cobbler.

RIMBONE // **That feeling you get when you see a**

beautiful set of rims. This can be either deep dish rims or handbuilt three-cross spoked wheels.

RODE LIKE A LION // The assertion that you rode like a Hardman.

RULE HOLISM // The notion of embracing The Rules in their entirety. The Rules are simultaneously simple and complex. They are consistent yet rife with contradiction. To embrace them all is to walk the path of La Vie Velominatus.

RULE V // Rule #5

RULE VV // Rule #10

THE RULES // The canon of cycling's etiquette. These are the simple truths of Cycling, compiled and maintained by the Velominati.

SCHLECKANICAL // Suffering an ill-timed mechanical during the height of competition. Extra points if the mechanical could possibly be the rider's own fault.

SCHLECKULATION // Speculation on how a rider will perform. Specifically as it related to predicting if a rider's less-than-stellar pre-TdF form foretells disaster or represents a ploy to fool rivals.

SHAVE HORIZONS // The boundary between smooth gun and hairy limb. Once you start shaving your legs, can you stop anywhere short of giving yourself a Brazilian, waxing your chest (men only, obviously), and shaving your eyebrows and head?

SILVER BULLETS // Silver cycling shoes.

SIT UP AND BEG // A high, upright riding position. The riding position of a cyclist whose bars are placed absurdly high.

SPINAL TAP BLACK // All black, all the time. When something can be none more black, like the colour of your cables, bars, saddle, tyres, or your soul.

SPRINTERS MUSCLE // The middle-aged male gut. The monolithic protuberance rising above one's waist and below one's rib cage which is a source of explosive power. Ironically, it is the opposite of a six pack but typically acquired by drinking beer.

STARTER PISTOLS // The Guns of Navarone in their primordial state.

STEERECTILE DYSFUNCTION // A large stack of spacers or a steep-angle stem. The inefficient and aesthetically displeasing setup leading to a Sit Up and Beg riding position. This also applies to any unnecessary stack of spacers piled above the stem, like some sort of Rule #45 safety-chute.

SUR LA PLAQUE // French for 'Put that thing in the Big Ring, fucktard.' Literally, to move Sur La Plaque means to move onto the plate, or the BIG RING.

SWITCHBONE // That feeling you get when you see a beautiful climb. The localised swelling resulting from looking at pictures of switchback-laden mountain passes like the Stelvio.

TAPERING // Not riding in preparation for a big ride. Refusing to do any ride of substance because one is Tapering to time one's peak. See also Train Properly and I Am Nearly Peaking.

THAT FUCKING BIKE // A derogatory slight to the Velominatus' tool, the bike. A Velominatus' domestic partner's reference to The Craft, who obviously does not understand The Work we do nor have any appreciation for Rule #11. A sample 'That Fucking Bike' conversation may be reviewed here.

THREE-POINT SYSTEM // The proper way to wear a hat. The system is a repeatable and reliable process to ensure you Look Fantastic wearing fundamentally ugly objects on your head: the front should be low to the eyes, sides running close to the ears, and the back no deviating below the nape of the neck.

TOAD HEAD // **Wearing the helmet too high upon the head.** The mushroom-like appearance of wearing a bicycle helmet too high upon the head.

TOO FAT TO CLIMB // **Being too heavy to climb well.** The assertion that one is overweight and will not be able to climb well. See also: related video.

TRAIN PROPERLY // **Controlling your pace when riding.** This figures heavily into the assertion that you are only being passed on a climb because you are following a strict training regimen.

THE V // **Old Velomiskrit for Rule #5.** This has evolved to take on the greater meaning it holds within the Velominati.

V AND VV // **Velomiskrit shorthand for Five and Ten.**

V-LOCUS // **The sacred point where rider and machine maximally channel The V.** The Italians call this la posizione. The Belgians call this 'riding your bike.'

V-METER // **The fictitious cylcometer which only reports on The V.** No confusing read-out. No buttons to push. No debate as to what you need to do. Just look down, ruminate briefly on the message conveyed to your oxygen-starved brain and lactate-laden legs, and V the fuck outa there. What's the gradient of the climb? V. How fast are you going? V. What's your heart rate doing? Your V-max? You will instantly and unequivocally know the answer.

VAMPIRE TACTICS // **Using a blood-doping ring to win bike races.**

VELOMIHOTTIE // **Velominata who is also a Velominatus' significant other.**

VELOMINADA // A Velominatus who has temporarily stopped riding. This is typically not due to any reduction in passion, but to outside factors that should be banished, like friends, family, or work.

VELOMINATA // Female cycling disciple of the highest order.

VELOMINATI // Plural form of Velominatus.

VELOMINATUS // A cycling disciple of the highest order.

VELOMINATUS BUDGETATUS // A Velominatus who finds great deals on expensive kit. This is a wily creature who always figures out a way to satiate the need for expensive kit using low-cost means.

VELOMINATUS VIOLATUS // A Velominatus who contravenes the Rules. Penance is paid in the form of hill repeats and heavy helpings of The V.

VELOMINAZI // A dogmatic enforcer of The Rules. This individual misinterprets the humor and intent behind The Rules and has likely missed their daily dose of humility and humor. They are also not likely to actually ride a bike very much or very well. See also: Adrian.

VELOMIWOOKIE // An unshaven Velominatus. After having failed to shave the guns, now sports a thatch that Chewbacca would be proud of.

VLVV // Velomiskrit shorthand for 'Vive la Vie Velominatus'.

VMH // Velomiskrit shorthand for Velomihottie. Velominata who also happens to be a Velominatus' significant other.

VONK // Failure to find your Rule #91 happy place.

THE V BANK // Some days you make deposits, other days you make withdrawals. But remember this: this is a bank with steep inactivity fees.

WELL HYDRATED // Consuming large quantities of alcohol (beer). This is usually after a ride in an effort to stay properly hydrated.

WHITE LADIES // White cycling shoes. Preferably made of patent-leather and by an Italian cobbler.

WOOKIE SHORTS // Shaving your guns to just above the tan line. This leaves furry patches above the shorts line that look like Chewbacca got stuck thigh-deep in a pool of Nair.

YELLOW JACKET OF AUTHORITY // A fluoro yellow wind/shower jacket. In the wild, this is sported by many commuting cyclists and gets its moniker from the smugness and perceived aura of invincibility that seems to emanate from wearers of this garish garment. Also comes in sleeveless version the YVA.

YELLOW PRINCESSES // Yellow cycling shoes. Made by the only company willing to do such a thing, Mavic.

YJA // Shorthand for Yellow Jacket of Authority.

Directory of The Rules

Rule #1 // Obey The Rules.

Rule #2 // Lead by example.

Rule #3 // Guide the uninitiated.

Rule #4 // It's all about the bike.

Rule #5 // Harden The Fuck Up.

Rule #6 // Free your mind and your legs will follow.

Rule #7 // Tan lines should be cultivated and kept razor sharp.

Rule #8 // Saddles, bars, and tyres shall be carefully matched.

Rule #9 // If you are out riding in bad weather, it means you are a badass. Period.

Rule #10 // It never gets easier, you just go faster.

Rule #11 // Family does not come first. The bike does.

Rule #12 // The correct number of bikes to own is n+1.

Rule #13 // If you draw race number 13, turn it upside down.

Rule #14 // Shorts should be black.

Rule #15 // Black shorts should also be worn with leader's jerseys.

Rule #16 // Respect the jersey.

Rule #17 // Team kit is for members of the team.

Rule #18 // Know what to wear. Don't suffer kit confusion.

Rule #19 // Introduce yourself.

Rule #20 // There are only three remedies for pain.

Rule #21 // Cold weather gear is for cold weather.

Rule #22 // Cycling caps are for Cycling.

Rule #23 // Tuck only after reaching Escape Velocity.

Rule #24 // Speeds and distances shall be referred to and measured in kilometres.

Rule #25 // The bikes on top of your car should be worth more than the car.

Rule #26 // Make your bike photogenic.

Rule #27 // Shorts and socks should be like Goldilocks.

Rule #28 // Socks can be any damn colour you like.

Rule #29 // No European posterior man-satchels.

Rule #30 // No frame-mounted pumps.

Rule #31 // Spare tubes, multi-tools and repair kits should be stored in jersey pockets.

Rule #32 // Humps are for camels: no hydration packs.

Rule #33 // Shave your guns.

Rule #34 // Mountain bike shoes and pedals have their place.

Rule #35 // No visors on the road.

Rule #36 // Eyewear shall be Cycling-specific.

Rule #37 // The arms of the eyewear shall always be placed over the helmet straps.

Rule #38 // Don't play leap frog.

Rule #39 // Never ride without your eyewear.

Rule #40 // Tyres are to be mounted with the label centered over the valve stem.

Rule #41 // Quick-release levers are to be carefully positioned.

Rule #42 // A bike race shall never be preceded with a swim and/or followed by a run.

Rule #43 // Don't be a jackass.

Rule #44 // Position matters.

Rule #45 // Slam your stem.

Rule #46 // Keep your bars level.

Rule #47 // Drink tripels, don't ride triples.

Rule #48 // Saddles must be level and pushed back.

Rule #49 // Keep the rubber side down.

Rule #50 // Facial hair is to be carefully regulated.

Rule #51 // Livestrong wristbands are cockrings for your arms.

Rule #52 // Drink in moderation.

Rule #53 // Keep your kit clean and new.

Rule #54 // No aerobars on road bikes.

Rule #55 // Earn your turns.

Rule #56 // Espresso or macchiato only.

Rule #57 // No stickers.

Rule #58 // Support your local bike shop.

Rule #59 // Hold your line.

Rule #60 // Ditch the washer-nut and valve-stem cap.

Rule #61 // Like your guns, saddles should be smooth and hard.

Rule #62 // You shall not ride with earphones.

Rule #63 // Point in the direction you're turning.

Rule #64 // Cornering confidence increases with time and experience.

Rule #65 // Maintain and respect your machine.

Rule #66 // No mirrors.

Rule #67 // Do your time in the wind.

Rule #68 // Rides are to be measured by quality, not quantity.

Rule #69 // Cycling shoes and bicycles are made for riding.

Rule #70 // The purpose of competing is to win.

Rule #71 // Train properly.

Rule #72 // Legs speak louder than words.

Rule #73 // Gear and brake cables should be cut to optimum length.

Rule #74 // V Meters or small computers only.

Rule #75 // Race numbers are for races.

Rule #76 // Helmets are to be hung from your stem.

Rule #77 // Respect the earth; don't litter.

Rule #78 // Remove unnecessary gear.

Rule #79 // Fight for your town lines.

Rule #80 // Always be Casually Deliberate.

Rule #81 // Don't talk it up.

Rule #82 // Close the gap.

Rule #83 // Be self-sufficient.

Rule #84 // Follow the Code.

Rule #85 // Descend like a Pro.

Rule #86 // Don't half-wheel.

Rule #87 // The ride starts on time. No exceptions.

Rule #88 // Don't surge.

Rule #89 // Pronounce it correctly.

Rule #90 // Never get out of the big ring.

Rule #91 // No food on training rides under four hours.

Rule #92 // No sprinting from the hoods.

Rule #93 // Descents are not for recovery. Recovery ales are for recovery.

Rule #94 // Use the correct tool for the job, and use the tool correctly.

Rule #95 // Never lift your bike over your head.

The Keepers of the Cog are:

// Frank Strack, Founder and Editor

A lifelong Velominatus, the history and culture within Cycling fascinates Frank (pronounced as the Dutch and Flemish *Frahnk*, not the American *Fraynk*) and, if given even the vaguest of excuses, will discuss it *ad nauseum*. A devoted Cycling aesthete, the only thing more important to him than riding a bike well is looking good doing it. Always humbly respectful of our heritage and healthily irreverent, his tongue-in-cheek attitude towards cycling belies his unyielding passion for it.

// Brett Kennedy, Founding Contributor / Editor

Whilst Brett hails from the land Down Under, he hates that fucking song. An Aussie now living as a Kiwi, he is at home on the rich dirt of New Zealand's mountain bike trails as he is on the scorching tarmac of Australia. Despite his geographical disadvantage, the cobblestones and kassien of Belgium and Northern France hold a special place in his heart and it's where you'll find him each Spring, either with a bike underneath him or a fine Belgian ale in his hand.

// John Andrews, Author

Gianni bought a champagne gold Peugeot with sew-up tyres in 1976. That was the beginning of the Troubles. Think Magnus Backstead without the big engine or rugged Swedish good looks. He has a small altar in his crawlspace containing smaller photos of Francesco Moser, Eros Poli and Gianni Bugno.

// Mark Carlson, Author

Marko lives and rides in the upper midwest of the States, Minnesota specifically. 'Cycling territory' and 'the midwest' don't usually end up in the same sentence unless the conversation turns to the roots of LeMond, Hampsten, Heiden and Ochowitz. While the pavé and bergs of Flanders are his preferred places to ride, you can usually find him harvesting gravel along forest and farm roads. He owes a lot to Cycling and his greatest contribution to the sport may forever be coining the term 'Rainbow Turd'.

// Jim Thomson, Author

Jim rides a bike a lot and hates people.

Join a literary community of like-minded readers who seek out the best in contemporary writing.

From the thousands of submissions Sceptre receives each year, our editors select the books we consider to be outstanding.

We look for distinctive voices, thought-provoking themes, original ideas, absorbing narratives and writing of prize-winning quality.

If you want to be the first to hear about our new discoveries, and would like the chance to receive advance reading copies of our books before they are published, visit

www.sceptrebooks.co.uk

 Follow @sceptrebooks

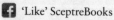 'Like' SceptreBooks

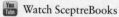 Watch SceptreBooks